LITTLE GOOD LUCK

A Memoir
by
Pamela Binns

Touring Japan we were always
having our fortunes told.
Mine was invariably *"Little good luck."*
An apt summary of my life.

CHAPTER ONE

In the beginning

June 2002

I lay for an awfully long time after the accident. The ambulance took ages. A stagehand (one I didn't know) supported me from behind. He kept whispering "sweet pea" in my ear – that was a comfort. And dear Michael and David sat where I could see them. They must have missed the whole of Act III.

We were actors in John Copley's iconic "La Bohème" – the wonderful production at the Royal Opera House. I was still wearing my Grisette dress from Act I, but I'd put my shawl over my head and secured it firmly with a nappy pin and taken off all my make-up to look like an old woman. We'd all been doing "Bohème" for years. At the call, Pauline Stroud (of "Lady Godiva Rides Again" fame) and I had left our dressing room in the bowels of the theatre. From the room next door, the children waved us off. "Break a leg!" they chanted. I went upstairs and did just that. We didn't know that, unexpectedly, the stage manager had lowered the floor backstage. We didn't know it could be lowered. It was all the new machinery that had just been installed in the Opera House's great makeover of 2000–2002. So I stepped out of the lift, into nothingness.

The pain was agonising. Pauline said, "Don't try to move. I think it's broken..." I already knew. Our dresser came with me in the ambulance – to bring the costume safely back to the Opera House. It had to be cut off. It must have been quite an entrance into St. Thomas' A&E. I heard a doctor say, "I'm going to knock you out for a minute, while I try to straighten your leg." He had to do it twice. Then I was sick. Someone else said, "I've got your brother on the phone. Would you like to speak to him?" As he'd barely made contact in the past twenty years, I was, to put it mildly, surprised. I think it was then that I lapsed into blessed unconsciousness.

When I came to, I was in a vast ward. Twenty beds, all of them occupied, ranged down each side. But I knew everything was going to be all right because smiling down were the two people who meant most to me – lovely Eileen Dodson and her daughter Sue. It didn't occur to me to ask how they knew where to find me. The great thing was, they were there. And Eileen was saying, "Don't worry, Pamela, I'm going to look after Mimi, just until you're well again." She made it sound like it was going to be a couple of weeks. That was Eileen all over. She also assured me that Alastair was going to take her to collect Mimi and then drive them back to her house in Fulham. (Eileen told me that for the moment my cat was being fed by the kind students in the flat above mine.) After they'd left I gazed at the flowers they'd brought. A beautiful little Victorian posy of white carnations ringed by pink rosebuds and some of those South African flowers that look like demented birds' heads. Sue had the sense to bring her own vases – she's a florist.

Apart from my flowers, there wasn't much else of comfort about the ward. The noise was deafening, overworked nurses hurried and scurried about, mostly bearing bedpans. I'd been offered some breakfast, which I didn't want, and someone had kindly given me a little emergency packet containing a toothbrush, toothpaste and a flannel. Later that first day my kind friend John Newbury brought a suitcase of things he'd collected from my flat. But right now I wanted to clean my teeth. My mouth felt disgusting, but the nurses seemed too busy to heed my calls, or my bell. I wished I'd asked Eileen or Sue... A nurse had come to me earlier, there'd been lots of questions about what I'd had for supper yesterday. With the number of times I'd been sick in A&E, the prawn salad I'd had before leaving for the theatre hardly seemed worth a mention. I felt shattered. I was bruised all over. I hardly dared to move my upper body or arms. My right leg, a vast yellow and black appendage, lay propped up on a pillow in front of me. A junior doctor came and squinted down at it. Mercifully he didn't attempt to handle or touch it. He told me they wouldn't be able to set it until some of the swelling came down. No one seemed to know how long that might take. A cheerful physiotherapist arrived, saying she was going to do just that. Reduce the swelling. Ominously she drew the curtains around my bed, assuring me it was going to be painful, but I could scream as loudly and as much as I liked. This became an extra daily agony to be endured, (of course without screaming, she was such a nice girl). I suggested arnica ointment – I'd used it all my life and knew how wonderfully effective it was for bruises. The girl thought this a brilliant idea. But she returned the next day, regretfully shaking her head. It seemed arnica was "alternative medicine" and the NHS doesn't do "alternative medicine." "Even though we both know it works?" I asked. That was a silly question.

For a few days I had a nice neighbour in the bed next to mine, but the population of this orthopaedic ward changed continually. The one constant was the old lady in the bed on my right. Day and night, every twenty minutes or so, there was a cry of, "Nurse, nurse, take me to the toilet." At first I was concerned, and rang my bell to get help for her. I was told to ignore her but this wasn't possible. Nor was sleep with her never-ending cries throughout the dark hours.

So, the days crawled by. We couldn't even buy a newspaper, apparently the boy couldn't make it up to the twelfth floor. I also heard that the lovely stagehand, who'd held me so wonderfully after the accident, had come to the hospital with a bunch of flowers. He wanted to know how I was getting on, and was turned away because he didn't know my name. (Years later, when I was working again at the Opera House, I was able to hug and thank him). Apart from being rude, this seemed a bit odd, as I gathered my fame had spread. Newcomers to the ward asked, "Which was the person who'd fallen off the stage at Covent Garden?" So sometimes I was pointed out as a visitor attraction. There was a huge plate glass window at the end of the ward, such a bonus for those lucky enough to have beds there. But for all of us, those who were compos mentis, watching Concorde go over morning and evening was a welcome diversion, and the other was watching a prisoner from the men's ward next to ours. The wretched man was taken, heavily chained to two warders, through the top of our ward to the adjoining loo. Imagination boggled at what happened when they reached their destination. The ladies' loo was always filthy, and became a slippery assault course for all on crutches. Unfortunately the Sister took a dislike to me from the moment I had the misfortune to arrive in her Ward. I don't know if this was because I was from the Opera House, or because I'm unlucky enough to have a voice that might be mistaken for the Upper Ten, I don't know. But this weaselly little woman nearly succeeded in making my life a complete misery. From the start when I was lying with my leg unset she decreed that I was to have neither bedpan nor commode. For me to have these was apparently "Unfair to the other occupants of the ward." (?) If I tried to stand unaided, the blood rushed down and the unwieldy appendage that my leg had become, swung about agonisingly and dangerously. I was saved by the kindness of several of the nurses, who managed to smuggle the necessities to me when Sister wasn't looking, and wonderful results can be achieved if you stop taking any liquid. Later, when I did begin wobbling my unsteady way to the loo on crutches, my journey was cheered on by some of the other more sympathetic patients. They knew I was struggling to survive. Two of the male nurses were especially kind. Don was very camp and after I'd let slip that I was once in the Dom Joly Show, as his Housekeeper, and that every other word I'd said was the "f..." one, he kept begging me to say it. As conditions in the ward deteriorated, I obliged with some vehemence. It made Don's day. Martin was gentler – he arranged surreptitious treats. Luckily we had no television in my ward. If that had been blaring all day we would have been in the bottom ring of purgatory. But when I was getting better, a couple of times Martin wheeled me to another ward for quick shots of my favourite vice – watching "Corrie". Another time he took me into the Day Room. He stationed my chair by the huge plate glass window and I had a wonderful quiet hour watching the Thames. I had no idea if I was looking up river or down – I've always been geographically dyslexic. But I didn't care, it was an hour of quiet calm after the hurly-burly of the ward.

At long last the day came when a junior doctor announced that my leg was ready for the setting operation. I was very relieved and the next day I went through all that. The following day he came to inspect his handiwork. He seemed pleased. He told me he'd been unable to remove the old metal plate in my leg that'd been there following a riding accident in my teens. He said he'd inserted a new plate just above it. Of course I had no idea how disastrous that was going to be in the not-so-distant future. I watched him amble away, thankful that my days in the ward must now be numbered.

I had many wonderful friends who visited and kept me going with encouragement and cheerfulness. But hardly anyone came in the evenings and that always seemed the loneliest time. Interminable hours stretched after the early supper to the final lowering of the ward lights. I would try to concentrate on a good book – but I looked longingly at the visitors clustered around other beds. But Dermot, the Chorus Manager from Covent Garden, who also looked after the actors, came one night. In fact he made two evening visits. I was very surprised to see him – I'd hardly ever met him when I was working at Covent Garden. Both times he came to tell me that I must sue the Opera House, which surprised me even more. He handed me a large box of chocolates and kept saying, "We were to blame!" It hadn't occurred to me that anyone was responsible for my accident. I hadn't realised that the Stage Manager should NOT have used the new machinery to lower the floor backstage without letting his action be generally known. I was gobsmacked at the news that I should sue the

Opera House. My mind raced through various scenarios of a packed courtroom where I pointed an accusing finger at Tony Hall (the Director of ROH, who I'd never even seen)... It all seemed so unlikely and in the end not at all dramatic. We never went to court. I would never have gone, anyway. The Opera House merely offered a modest sum of compensation, which I accepted. Meanwhile, here at my bedside, conversation languished. Luckily it turned out that Dermot had a cat. (I gather it joined the Great Purr in the sky shortly afterwards). But that evening Cat Talk kept us both going. Some years later, when I was back working at The Garden, Dermot called out to me across the crowded coffee lounge, "How's your pussy?" Cue merriment among the actors. Dermot's second visit was easier. He brought me a nice bottle of wine, which of course I wasn't allowed to consume until I returned to civilisation, and repeated his message about suing the Opera House. He said he'd send the Equity Deputy to help me. This time he came with a friend, which made talking easier. They were going on to "The Faery Queen" at the Coly.

Dermot was as good as his word and two days later David Evans Rees arrived at my bedside. He brought with him the portable telephone machine, which he'd nabbed from a neighbouring ward, and a large supply of pound coins. He dialled Equity's number and I had to tell them about the accident, which I found appallingly difficult. I never knew which way I had turned out of the lift, though the fearsome young female solicitor appointed to handle my case questioned me so often and so brutally I was frequently reduced to tears. "I'm only preparing you for being cross-questioned in court!" she'd say, always ignoring my oft repeated retort that if it came court I was going to forget the whole thing. This disagreeable young woman also reduced my dear friends Eileen and Pauline to tears with her questioning, and then, but I'm jumping ahead a few years, when I was nearly better, she suddenly wrote and said that she was giving up my case and leaving the firm of solicitors. I noted that she neither wished me a return to health nor good luck with the case, which was then taken over by one of the firm's senior directors, a gentleman with exquisite manners who quietly and calmly saw the whole matter settled to everyone's satisfaction.

Meanwhile, the telephone machine ate up an enormous amount of pound coins and left me exhausted after trying to give a coherent account of what happened. But it must have been all right, because from then on, thanks to Dermot and David, Equity looked after me quite wonderfully. They appointed and paid for this firm of solicitors to handle my case. For the first year I also received financial support from Equity's own insurance company.

But I was terribly worried about being discharged from the hospital. It looked as if it was never going to happen. I felt I was in for a life sentence and was going to live on the ward forever. By this time I had struggled with walking on crutches and had become fairly proficient – on the flat. But the short flight of steps we were required to go up (and down) was definitely a no-no. The great plaster now encasing my right leg was just too heavy and swung about uncontrollably as I tried to mount with just my left leg and the crutches. The weaselly Sister, aware of my difficulties, decreed that I could not be discharged until I had mastered the step climbing. Both up and down, she insisted. I was in despair, since I knew I couldn't to do it until the plaster was removed.

Completely desperate, I managed to get hold of the telephone machine. I rang Denville Hall, the Actors' Retirement Home near Northwood. I'd had a sojourn there a few years earlier, when I was recovering from a failed knee operation. The principal, Mrs Miller, had always been very kind to me. On this occasion, I managed to speak to her on the phone. After outlining my plight, she promised to see what she could do. She was as good as her word. When I next rang she told me she had a room for me and would order an ambulance as soon as I was ready to leave.

"As soon as...?" I could hardly believe my ears or my lucky stars. I alerted my kind friends among the nurses and all was arranged. My belongings were packed and I was off. I had a last view of the Ward. Sister Weasel was running between the beds screaming, "She's going private! She's going private! And I wasn't even told..."

CHAPTER TWO

2002

After the bleakness of the Ward, I was engulfed by kindness on my arrival at Denville Hall. The staff there are wonderful and stay for years. Many of them remembered me from my previous visit and embraced me warmly. And you are well looked after by the nursing staff, too. I was given such a pretty room, with pink roses on the curtains and wallpaper. I was told that it had previously been occupied by Pat Coombs.

Though chiefly known as a brilliant comedienne, Pat also did some work as a straight actress. We'd been together in the BBC television classic serial of "Cranford" in 1972. Pat was a lovely person, though I remember at that time she was very depressed after an unhappy love-affair. "It'll all come right. I know it will," she kept repeating. And I admired her for this, though as I knew the actor concerned, I rather doubted a happy outcome. "Cranford" had a wonderful part for me – I played Jessie Brown, the juvenile lead, with a chance to act the great Victorian death-bed scene, when my elder sister, brilliantly portrayed by Freda Dowie, passed away. I was so proud when Ronald Culver, who was our Dad, confessed that I'd made him blub as he watched the recording. Freda was lovely too. She brought me lots of little vegetable cuttings from her garden in the country for me to grow on my London balcony.

There was one cloud shortly after my happy arrival at Denville. A friend of long-standing, Magdalen Egerton, was also recovering there following a triple heart-bypass operation. Never the most tactful of people, Magda barged into my room and announced that a dear friend of ours, John Iball, had just died. It seemed she would be going to the funeral. In fact, for someone who'd just had a big operation, she appeared remarkably fit and healthy. She was always going off (in a taxi) to the fleshpots of Northwood. I was wheelchair bound and not able to go anywhere. All I could do was send a cheque to the Macmillan Nurses who helped so much with John's long fight with throat cancer. And, of course, all my love and sympathy to Alastair, his partner.

The one drawback to Denville was its inaccessibility. As visitors discover, it's a very long way from Northwood station. But when my lovely friend Eileen came to visit me she wasn't put off by a little thing like that. She hitched a lift on the Florist's van. That was a red letter day. Sometimes the hours dragged interminably. The stars living at Denville tended to be snooty and kept themselves to themselves. Once I was sitting opposite Peggy Mount, now completely blind. Suddenly she boomed, "D'you know, there are some people here who don't pay?!" Being one of them, I winced visibly. Seeing my expression, her neighbour shut Peggy up. Then there was John Barron, lording it over his own table with his own bottle of wine. I'd worked for him briefly, at Wolverhampton. Giving notes to the company he'd alluded to me as "the little genius" – a reference to my notice in the local rag. This didn't seem a time to remind him of our acquaintance long ago. But some of the other thespians staying there were more friendly.

There was a wonderful story about Betty Driver, moving in to retire permanently at Denville. All day long she ordered the removal men to rearrange the furniture she'd brought with her – "The chest a little to the left – then that chair can go in there…No, that's not right. Let's try it as it was before – put the picture a bit higher so the vase can fit in underneath…" At the end of the day, exhausted, Betty repaired to the bar. She ordered a double gin, climbed onto the bar, said "Bottoms up!" and dropped down dead! Oh, to go just like that…

But sometimes there was a definite air of being back at school, with Mrs. Miller as the Head Mistress. One morning there were notes from her on our morning breakfast trays. Everyone at Denville has breakfast in bed – one of the happiest traditions of the place. This morning we were sternly admonished that she'd heard malicious rumours circulating among the residents that the standard of the meals was deteriorating. I was gobsmacked, I thought the food served at Denville was wonderful. Far too good, in fact, and far too much of it. I'd already noticed that I was putting on weight. And I hadn't heard anyone else complaining. But here was this note and we were all ordered to present ourselves in the bar at 11 o'clock sharp.

So dutifully we all assembled, the stars and the lesser thesps like Magda and me. And goodness, did we receive a telling off from teacher? If we had complaints, (well, I hadn't) we weren't to whisper among ourselves, we were to go straight to her, Mrs. Miller, at once, and she would investigate. Then there was something about there having been a bit of trouble with the deputy Chef, but I'd lost interest...

I was more concerned about my weight gain. Luckily my skirts had elastic waists, but I'd burst out of my bras and had to discard them. There was a lovely lady, also called Pamela, who came round the Hall once a week to ask if we wanted any shopping. I beseeched her to find me a bigger bra and she produced the best Northwood could offer. But she could find nothing to fit me. So there was no alternative but to stop wearing one. Of course, as soon as I got home and returned to iron rations, the weight I'd gained at Denville dropped off.

Before I left, I had to return to St. Thomas' for a routine appointment to check how I was getting on. Once more the long journey by ambulance and all the endless waiting in the queue for an x-ray. The progress of my leg, still in the heavy plaster, was pronounced satisfactory. (The operation had been done by a very junior doctor.) That day I was actually seen by the head orthopaedic surgeon. I plucked up courage and told him that my shoulder was still painful from the accident, in fact it hurt far more than my leg. He said he'd give me a steroid injection. I was taken behind a screen and the nurse told me to take off my T-shirt. Viewing my bra-less state, she all but fainted. "Really, Miss Binns, I never thought you were the Women's Lib lot – burning your bra an' all that –." Her exclamations of horror were cut short by the arrival of the surgeon. I was hastily made decent with a draped towel. The injection I was given actually worked. My shoulder was frozen for a few days, but after that there was no more pain.

Shortly after my hospital visit, the medical staff at Denville decided that I was well enough to go home. I was both excited and full of fear about how I was going to manage. On the flat I could hop about confidently, but I still couldn't do stairs. This was going to make life in my little flat difficult. I live in a converted Victorian house and I'm on the second floor. Unfortunately my kitchen, off the living room, is up six fairly steep steps, but once again Mrs. Miller organised things for me. She got in touch with Social Services and Westminster carers were booked to come in three times a day to look after me.

I needn't have worried about the fifty stairs up to my flat – the kind ambulance men carried me up as if I was a fluff of thistledown – not the heaviest I'd been for years. And that evening I met Yvonne – a vast seventeen-stone black lady who was to be my principal carer. The wonderful John Newbury, who lived ten minutes away and was to give me such unfailing support, had been shopping and got in bread and milk and eggs. I suggested to Yvonne a boiled egg might do for my supper. After the rich food at Denville everything was going to change. But a look of complete incomprehension registered on Yvonne's broad face. No cook myself, I patiently outlined to Yvonne (John always called her Why-vonne and the name stuck) how to boil an egg. The operation took half an hour. But I didn't care. I was back in my own flat and full of hope and optimism. Surely my leg would have set by Christmas? And then I'd be able to resume my normal life as an actress. Yvonne (I hope you're now thinking of her as Why-vonne) served the egg, hard as a bullet and still in its shell, on a saucer, with a fork to eat it. I managed to get it down and Yvonne announced she was off now. So no hope of any help with my unpacking and getting into bed.

Things weren't much better in the morning. I woke early, with a parched throat and I couldn't get up to the kitchen (because of the six stairs) to make a cup of tea. Or even a drink of water – the drinking water came from the kitchen tap. Later I managed to organise bottles of drinking water in the two rooms I occupied and later still, with Eileen's help, a Thermos of tea (to be prepared by an unwilling carer) by my bed. Almost the toughest lesson I had to learn was being dependent on other people for almost everything. I'd always been independent and I found it hard. But that first morning I had to discover how much I could do on my own. Balancing carefully on my crutches, I managed to drag the coronation stool from the hall into the bathroom. Seated in front of the basin, I managed a strip wash and cleaning my teeth. Back in the bedroom (and Yvonne would have to replace the stool later) I struggled to dress – a skirt and T-shirt were all I could manage. With Yvonne's cooking, or rather lack of it, I was soon able to wear bras again. She turned up at ten thirty and served some cereal for my breakfast, reluctantly she made my bed. She didn't reappear till the evening. But I was lucky that day – around two-ish another carer appeared and was able to rustle up some salad for lunch. I survived this strange regime of the carers not turning up almost entirely because of the devotion of John and Eileen. John managed to come round on so many days – always asking what I needed and ready to execute any number of errands. And Eileen came over for a day every week from her home in Fulham. She'd bring a picnic lunch – usually ham rolls and eclairs. But before we devoured them she'd set to and clean the flat –she scrubbed the kitchen floor and regularly defrosted the fridge. The carers would do none of these things, they said it wasn't in their remit. To give them their due, they really didn't have time – they were allotted no travelling time – one could leave me at 11.30 a.m. and be expected to be at her next job in Holborn at the same hour! Eileen chatted away nineteen to the dozen while she did these chores. I so longed to join in and help – I felt so useless just sitting in my chair. But I was always doing my exercises and every day my leg was getting stronger and more mobile. Then, after the picnic lunch Eileen brought and much laughter, we'd start on The Times easy crossword. Eileen was a crossword fanatic, any paper she found left on a train she's be searching for the puzzle page and starting the crossword. She'd left school at fourteen and started working in Barker's Accounts Department under a martinet manager. She wasn't good at maths and came home every night in tears, until her father bought her a ready reckoner. She quickly learnt to use this and then it was smiles all the way. She often said she wished she was still working and was envious that, as an actor, I would be able to go on and on. But we were a good combination for crosswords: I knew most of the literary quotes and allusions, Eileen was a whizz at the cryptic word clues. Sometimes we even finished The Times easy one.

All too soon it would be time for Eileen to leave, sensibly she liked to go in time to miss the rush hour. She'd have a final tidy up and collect my dirty washing, which, God bless her, she took every week and put through her machine. Then it was time to say goodbye and I would try not to be tearful…Eileen was still looking after Mimi, but she promised to bring her back to me soon.

For my leg really was getting better. With help from my aged physiotherapist, I was slowly, slowly – managing the fifty stairs down from my flat. It was the greatest day when I finally made it to the front door and stepped out into the fresh air. (Alas, I couldn't get onto my own balcony because of the steps up to the kitchen – where the door is.) The next day, with a few more tentative steps, I made it to the front gate. Soon, I was on the pavement and going up the road. And as the strength in my leg returned my confidence grew. On one of my monthly visits to St. Thomas' the plaster had been removed. The head orthopaedic surgeon, who hadn't done the setting, deigned to speak to me. "I see you've been released," he observed. Oh, the bliss of being able to scratch as long and hard as I wished, instead of poking ineffectually down the plaster with a knitting needle.

And Eileen did bring Mimi back, though it wasn't a day of general rejoicing. Mimi, who'd had nothing but TLC from the day of her birth, was a nervous, highly-strung cat. The moment Eileen let her out of the basket, she dived under my bed and refused to come out. I didn't see her again till past midnight, when she suddenly jumped back onto my bed and we had a great purring reunion. But Eileen had also come to say goodbye – in a few days' time she was flying to Australia to spend four months with her son and his family. I tried not to cry when she left, but my life was going to be awfully empty without her telephone calls and weekly visits. But having my lovely tabby back helped.

In mid-December I was walking with two sticks and had been told my leg was now set – completely weight bearing. I was used to going up the road alone. I decided to post my Christmas cards. I put them in a satchel, slung over my shoulder. The pillar box was two streets away. Cards safely posted, I turned away. As I turned, something in my leg gave way. There was a searing pain – and in that second I knew it had broken again. So I stood on the road, gasping at the pain, but supported by my two sticks. I tried to take a few tentative steps – the pain was horrendous. I looked up and down the road; it was completely deserted. Usually at that time there were dog walkers and mothers with small children and buggies. Somehow, and I've no idea how long it took me, I managed to get back to the house. I hitched up the fifty stairs on my bottom. It always amazed me that I hadn't met a single soul on that tortuous journey. If I had, I suppose I would have asked them to call an ambulance and my life would have turned out rather differently. Eventually I got home.

After I'd recovered a bit, I managed to find my crutches – they were the first things I needed. A strong drink didn't come amiss, either. Hot sweet tea would probably have been better, but this was no time for niceties. Then I rang my GP – the Receptionist was frosty (for many years she'd pretended not to know me.) "Get yourself to St. Charles' and get it x-rayed" she instructed. "I can't," I said. "It's broken..." She put the phone down. By then I was too exhausted to try any more. I managed to feed Mimi and lay on the bed. After a long time and despite the pain, I slept.

By the next day a huge lump had appeared on my leg. I supposed it had calcified. I rang the

leg, now encased in bright pink plaster, which had been put on before I left King's, swinging about helplessly as I moved. And carers coming twice a day, three times if I was lucky. I wrote a story around the happenings of my awful Christmas Day. A long time later John typed it out for me and I sold it to a magazine.

We were just into the New Year, 2003, when, early one morning, I had a telephone call from King's College Hospital. They said they were sending an ambulance for me at two o'clock and I was to pack a suitcase immediately. I simply couldn't understand it – Mr. Groom had said he would operate on January 10th – more than a week away. Perhaps they wanted me for tests, or for a pre-op medical? I had no option but to summon the faithful John to pack my suitcase and await developments.

And what developments! I was deposited in the NHS quarter of King's. (I already understood, courtesy of some kindness and the Insurance, that from now on I was going private.) No one seemed to be expecting me, or to know what to do with me. I was put into a small room with two beds and left sitting on a hard chair for some hours. One or two people popped in from time to time and asked for my particulars. I answered their questions and everything I said seemed to mystify them further. My painkillers, were, of course, in my unopened suitcase. The pain in my leg, hanging down as it was, increased with every minute that passed. So I pleaded with the next person who came. She was Japanese and seemed to be a junior doctor. Finally she did produce some white tablets and a glass of water. She also said that no one had any idea why I'd been sent for and admitted. I swallowed the tablets gratefully and they did help to dull the pain. After the little Japanese lady had gone, no one came near me for a further hour. My next visitor was a very large black lady bearing a plastic bowl. Obviously a dame of few words, she shoved it at me, muttering, "Yer supper," and withdrew. The bowl contained a brown mess resembling some kind of animal food, except that Mimi wouldn't have touched it. (I'd arranged for the kind students in the flat above to look after her, pro tem.)

I transferred the bowl to the floor, a tricky operation for me, and was interrupted by the arrival of two young men. I couldn't decide whether they were medical students or very junior doctors. But at least they seemed cheerful. They sat themselves, together, on one of the beds, facing me.

"No one seems to know why you're here..." said One. The other giggled and managed, "We think there's been a terrible mistake." My line of thought for the last three hours. But number One went on, "Typical of this place..." Number Two took up the story. They really were like Tweedledee and Tweedledum, "You're Mr. Groom's patient, we gather and he's going to operate on you on the 10th?" By now I was so worn out and tired I could only nod my head. I was long past speech.

The double act leapt to their feet. "We're

going to ring him up. He's on holiday in the South of France." They bounded towards the door with the energy of extreme youth, but turned to say, "He's going to be awfully cross about this!" This thought seemed to amuse them, they left, helpless with giggles.

They returned in a remarkably short time. They were almost whooping with glee at the news they had to impart.

"We got him. Just starting his dinner – with oysters." I could vaguely imagine the scene. "He was furious! And when he's angry like that." Number One paused for the dramatic effect. Number Two carried on, "You being brought in today is just one ghastly mistake! We're to apologise on behalf of King's."

"He's looking forward to seeing you on the 10th," from number One. And with more laughter and apologies, they left. Very soon the mighty hospital bureaucratic system swung into action. An authoritative man appeared and announced I was being sent home immediately.

"Oh no, I'm not!" I said firmly. In the last half-hour I'd begun to anticipate this development. I continued, "It's ten o'clock at night. I live alone. The flat will be dark and deserted..." (I seemed to have said this somewhere before. It was becoming my mantra.)

I had to do quite a lot more arguing. It seemed King's didn't want to go to all the trouble of admitting me and then having to fill in all my discharge papers the next morning. But I remained adamant. I'd had my eye on the bed for some time and once all the tiresome formalities had been completed I managed to climb in. It was unspeakable bliss to be lying flat with my legs up and a nurse even came and unpacked my night things. I put them on and clambered out to clean my teeth. There was no plug for the basin. I managed to sleep a little.

And in the morning, after all the business of being formally discharged had been completed and the usual long wait, I was sent home in another ambulance.

CHAPTER THREE

2003

I waited patiently, or as patiently as my restricted life allowed, for the next move towards regaining the use of my right leg.

On January 9th 2003, I was taken by ambulance to the rather swish entrance to the private wing at King's. I had to wait ages for someone with a wheelchair to take me up to my room, which was really rather nasty. All the private rooms at King's face onto blank walls. Hardly inspiring. At least I was alone and could be miserable in comfort. I settled in with my pile of books and my radio, and a photo of Mimi.

Mr. Groom came to see me in the evening and was very affable. But he didn't tell me what he intended to do in the operation. I saw him very briefly the next day, just before I went under. He was already gowned-up and wearing a J-cloth rakishly round his head. He told me he was going to sprinkle "fairy dust" on my leg to help the healing. Much later I learnt this "dust" came from France and cost £2,000! Of course I didn't pay – but "fairy dust" was a comforting thought as I fell asleep.

This was to be about my fourteenth operation. I'd started at four, having my tonsils and adenoids out. I was traumatised by the whole business. Nanny was with me, sharing my room, but I quite desperately wanted Marje, my mother, who never came to the hospital. But after that experience I've always managed coming round from operations beautifully – (mental preparation beforehand) and then coming up, up like a bird... and NEVER being sick.

Alas, my first experience at King's was quite different. I was in this horrid little room and there were lots of people crowding round the bed. Someone told me, if the pain was bad, I was to squeeze the thing on my right shoulder. As the pain in my right leg was raging right through me, I pressed this rubber bulb and promptly I was sick. I couldn't understand the terrible pain in my leg, which didn't seem to be in plaster. Something hard, like iron, was encasing it. I tried to explore with my good leg, but I couldn't make sense of anything. The pain was overwhelming. I pressed the thing on my shoulder and again was sick. From then on it became a routine – press-sick...press-sick...press-sick. I tried to speak to someone in the crowd round my bed, but I was always sick before I could frame any words. Then suddenly a tall man in white stepped forward and dragged me out of bed. He seemed to be saying, "Stand up! Stand straight!" I screamed. Now I knew it was all a nightmare and I had to wake up. Consumed by pain I crumpled and was sick again. The next thing I knew I was being lifted back into bed by a very large woman, who looked like a Red Indian. I learnt later she was the

Sister of the private wing. A really kind lady – if you kept on the right side of her. "I'm removing the morphia" – so that was the bell-push thing on my shoulder. "It doesn't agree with you. I'll send Nurse with some painkillers…" her gentle voice belied her stern appearance.

For a few minutes the room was empty. I managed to reach for a tissue and mop my poor sodden face. I tried to breathe with and through the pain. But where was the plaster? Tentatively I explored down my leg. It seemed to be being held in an iron frame and oh, the horror, spikes from it seemed to go right through the bones of my leg and come out the other side… I'd just about taken all this in when a dear little nurse appeared with ordinary painkillers and a glass of water to wash them down. Once I'd taken those she mopped me up and tried to make me more comfortable. She even asked if I was hungry. (I'd had a long 'Nil By Mouth' wait before the operation. But her suggestion now would just have brought on more sickness.) I plucked up enough courage to ask about the strange contraption on my leg.

"Oh, that's an Ilizarov frame –" she said airily. "It's the modern way of setting bones. They do much better than in plaster." At that point I groaned. "Didn't anyone tell you that you were having one?" I shook my head. "You'll soon get used to it. You'll soon be hopping about!" At that point hopping about seemed completely unlikely. I asked about the man who'd dragged me out of bed. "He's a physiotherapist. You'll be seeing a lot more of him.

It's hospital policy to get patients on their feet immediately after the operation. But obviously you weren't up to it..." At that moment any thought of any further movement seemed unlikely. Luckily I soon feel asleep.

A week or two later, together with other leg sufferers from the Lindo Wing, I was taken in a wheelchair to a room in the hospital for a special film show. The film was all about Mr. Ilizarov's invention of the frames that were encasing the legs of all present. We were shown lots of merry patients from what looked a cosy clinic, gambolling about in deep snow. In Russia, I presumed. With great glee they were hurling snowballs at each other. I looked round at my fellow patients, every face was glum. I didn't think there was going to be much gambolling or snowballing in the corridors at King's. I noticed everyone in the film was putting their full weight on their injured leg. Throughout the three and a half years of my imprisonment, I wasn't able to put my right leg to the ground, let alone stand on it. But hats off to you, comrade Ilizarov, for your wonderful invention. It took a long time and much reconstructive surgery but eventually my leg set beautifully.

Sister Debbie, Mr. Groom's nurse, visited me regularly. She was a wonderful person and so helpful with nearly all the problems, large and small, that I faced. First of all she taught me to clean the frame. This had to be done every day and took about an hour. I had to tell the nurses when I was ready to do it and they would bring all the things to my bedside. Where every pin went in (and came out) was 'open' and liable to bleed, so everything had to be kept sterile. Cleaners were not allowed into my room while I was doing it – so that no dust was raised. Each side of each pin had to be meticulously cleaned on both sides of the leg, with a tissue, before a final wipe everywhere of the strong disinfectant. Of course I wore disposable gloves. I had to continue doing this every day once I got home, and there it was difficult to keep everything sterile. In fact I had an infection – that they were never able to trace – in my leg, for the greater part of the three years. I was almost continually taking some quite filthy antibiotics, which produced instant diarrhoea. But then, at least, I could take the constipating painkillers.

One day, Debbie brought me a booklet, "Living With Your Frame." I quickly turned to the section on "Knickers." Since the barrel of iron had been attached to my right leg, I hadn't been able to get any on. The booklet said it was perfectly possible to wear them with your Ilizarov. The secret, it seemed, was to get a friend to cut and open up old pairs and affix several Velcro straps to each side and voila! My friend Magda, who was something of a seamstress, volunteered for the job.

I didn't try them till I got home. I was lying on the bed and managed to get my left leg through the proper hole easily enough. But I couldn't stand without support. So, I went back to lying down and with much wriggling, managed to get the open part of the pants round me. Triumphantly I did up the

Velcro. But every time I reached for my crutches and stood up, the pants descended round my ankles. I gave up and just went "Knickerless to King's."

A long, long time later, my friend Pauline solved the problem. I don't know where she found them, but she produced three pairs of huge boxer shorts. The leg holes were big enough to go over the offending frame. I still felt like one of those criminals of old who'd been soldered into their irons, but at least decency now prevailed.

So, back to my stay in the Lindo Wing. Mr. Groom came to visit me quite often and always said I was making good progress. He was cheerful as well as caring and admired Mimi's photo, which I'd stuck on the wall so that I could see her from the bed. Mr. Groom's wildly attractive assistant Sam, came every day. Pauline was mad for him. He explained to me what a difficult time Mr. Groom had had with my operation. He'd had to dig out not only the plate St. Thomas' had put in my leg, but the old one beneath it from the riding accident I'd had at fifteen. Sam said I'd been lucky to get that old one put in, as, at that time, Mr. Leather at the Birmingham Accident Hospital where I was taken, was the only surgeon setting bones like that.

Sam knew all about my leg snapping under me out in the road. He said whoever operated on me at St. Thomas' should have got the old plate out, even if it had taken four hours. "If they'd run a metal rod from just above your ankle to just below your knee you'd have been fine," concluded Sam.

And it was Sam who became concerned I wasn't eating enough. We got the menu every day, but the food was hardly gourmet. I kept asking for sandwiches, the only thing I fancied. And by the time they came I'd gone off the whole idea of eating. The nursing was mostly good, but there were exceptions. I've never been a good sleeper, ever since the year I spent in plaster after the riding accident, long ago. Insomnia is an old familiar friend. Mr. Groom, always sympathetic, prescribed strong sleeping tablets for me. They were very effective, when they came. Their delivery, together with my other evening medication, became more and more hazardous. One night I lay rigid and sleepless, listening to the desolate booming sound that came every few minutes. I think it must have been other patient's bells but to me it seemed like the call of a lighthouse, far out among the rocks. Sometimes, even now, when I'm sleepless at home in my own dear little bed, I hear that dreadful sound and I'm back in the Lindo Wing, a washed-up distressed vessel, beached among the other wrecks...On that particular night my sleeping pills came at 3 a.m. When Mr. Groom popped in for his morning visit I told him why I was bleary-eyed and not feeling too good. But I wasn't prepared for his anger. He simply left the room and exploded. I heard him bellowing all the way down the corridor to the Nursing Station. That evening the Red Indian Sister brought my pills herself at six o'clock, before she went off duty. "It's been decided," she said quietly, "It'll be best for you to have your tablets before the day staff go off. Then you can take them yourself when you want to put your light out." Thank you, Mr. Groom.

The physiotherapists came every day. They were tough – they needed to be. The horrendous incident of the one who tried to haul me out of bed immediately after the operation was never mentioned. I worked hard, I wanted to get better and go home. On my crutches, I ploughed my way up and down the corridors on the afternoons I didn't have visitors. (My friends were so good about coming.) My right leg still swung about, but not as violently as it had in plaster. I was getting used to the frame (but not sleeping on my back and being unable to turn over). I even began to attempt the stairs, everyone was very encouraging about my efforts and hard work.

At last the day came when I was discharged. I was now a bit more secure at walking on my crutches, (no weight on the right leg, of course) but still quite unable to mount the fifty stairs to my flat. Or even the six ones that led to my kitchen. So I was once more a prisoner, quite unable to get myself a cup of tea, and completely at the mercy of the carers supplied by Westminster Council. Three were supposed to come each day, but rarely did. They served meals – of sorts, and did one hour's shopping a week. About halfway through my three-year sentence, Westminster suddenly decided to assess me and from then on I had to pay for the carers. In order to keep track of the service I received, I drew a grid of twenty-one squares for each week and marked off each time a carer turned up. I thought Westminster couldn't dispute such evidence when the time came to send the cheque each month, but they did, they did. People asked how I filled my days, but by the time I'd cleaned the Ilizarov frame, done my exercises, thought what I could have for my few little meals and argued with Westminster over the amounts I owed, the days passed. I did some bits of writing and lovely John Newbury was kind enough to type out my efforts. I even sold some of the stories and articles. But my opera book, about my life at Covent Garden, which I worked on all the time, I wasn't able to place. Despite the most encouraging letter I received from Penelope Hoare, the renowned editor, after she'd read the manuscript.

I had great sympathy with the carers and realised they had no time to do housework, really no time to do anything except serve my scanty meals.

I had wonderfully cheerful letters from Eileen in Australia, but I missed her dreadfully. I gradually grew tired and weaker with the poor food I was getting. The carers were only allotted one hour a week to shop for me and most of them couldn't cook anyway. Eileen, on her weekly visits, had always brought food and at least one proper meal. One evening, a nice black girl came down from the kitchen and told me there was nothing she could prepare for my supper. "Isn't there a tin of something?" I asked hopefully. I heard various crashing sounds, which showed she was searching. She came down again to me in my chair, my leg was propped up in front of me. "There's only this." She held out a dusty and dented tin. I squinted at it. It was no longer labelled, but from the shape I guessed it must be either tuna or salmon. The sell-by date was obliterated by grime. "Oh, that'll do," I said, and added hopefully, "Could you put it on some toast...?" So that was supper settled. Whatever had been in the tin tasted a bit odd. But with all the medication I had to take, so did so many things. Everything about my life seemed odd at this time.

It wasn't until the following evening that I began to feel peculiar. Very hot. All over. Everywhere. Both my legs were burning. The injured one felt as if it was on fire. It was the riding accident of my youth all over again. I longed for a cool stream or river. Or to step into the healing power of the sea. I desperately needed to toss and turn. But imprisoned in an Ilizarov frame you have to lie on your back. It's not even possible to turn onto your side. I was used to sleeping on my back, but this was something different. Vaguely I realised I was ill. I got worse. I supposed I had a fever. With frequent and agonising trips to the bathroom becoming ever more necessary, I supposed I had food poisoning. In the short periods between, when I managed to get back into bed, I realised I needed help. Another person. Someone to help me. Someone to come and do all the right things. I'd dropped the address book, with all my friend's numbers, and couldn't bend down to reach it. The telephone, beside my bed, now seemed a hundred miles away. In some other world. As I was. I'd gone too far now to summon help. I was floating somewhere where no one could reach me. I don't know if any carers came during that strange time. I was beyond buzzers or opening the door. (Since nearly every visit brought a different carer, it was not possible for them all to have the keys.)

Strange things were happening in the place I'd gone to. There were three soldiers in battle dress, coughing and choking, as they fought their way through the thick fog that also engulfed me. I watched them emerge through it, whole and jubilant. I so wanted to join them, but slowly and painfully I returned to my own bed. A long time later I learned that the date was March 3rd 2003. The Iraq war had started and the first three soldiers had been killed in action. I always so wanted to tell the relatives what I'd seen.

Gradually I grew cooler and cooler. I went to the bathroom for the thousandth time. Exhausted and about to try to make the return journey to my bed, my crutches slipped on the wet floor. My one supporting leg went from under me and, as I fell over backwards, I heard something crack. I knew at once one of the pins inside the bone had snapped. The pain was blinding and it seemed unlikely I'd ever get back on my one leg again. But there was no one to help me get up. Through sheer necessity, hanging for dear life on to the side of the bath, I managed to get myself upright. I felt about for my fallen crutches and eventually made it back to bed.

In the morning, I managed to ring Debbie, Mr.

Groom's wonderful Sister. At last I had a bit of luck, there was a Clinic the next day. Debbie said she'd arrange an ambulance for me.

The following morning there was the usual agonising wait for it to arrive. I had to be ready by 7 a.m. in case, by any miraculous chance, it came early. As I couldn't get up the six stairs to the kitchen, it wasn't possible to get myself anything to eat or drink. Which was just as well, since as I always went to the hospital alone, there was no one to help me go to the loo. I couldn't bother the nurses, they were all far too busy. I just had to wait and make-do somehow, until I was delivered home in the evening. When the ambulance did eventually arrive, they always said they'd been given the wrong address and they'd been searching for me all over London. So every time I rang "Transport" at King's, I tried to get this put right. They never listened, but always said, "Oh, yes, Miss Binns, we've got your address correctly ..." And so the mistakes continued.

But on this particular morning the tumbril did appear in pretty good time. On arrival at the hospital I was hoisted into a wheelchair, and after a quick word with the ever-smiling Debbie, I joined the everlasting queue for x-rays. Then it was a long time to wait before it was my turn in Mr. Groom's inner sanctum. By then he'd seen the new x-rays. Debbie was in attendance, waiting to see what needed to be done. Instead of cracking his usual jokes, Mr. Groom just held my hand and said, "I'm so sorry." As I'd thought, one of the pins was broken inside the bone. He was going to have to break my leg all over again and re-set it with a new Ilizarov frame. He tried to be cheerful, but all I could think of was the long months stretching ahead. Would I ever walk properly and be free again? Mr. Groom added that there was a great protuberance of bone on one side, and he'd be able to remove that and improve the appearance of my leg. I'd noticed that, but I was past caring what my leg looked like, just as long as it worked, as a leg. Mr. Groom also said that my leg had shortened but they'd be able to lengthen it, and get it back level with my left one. I didn't realise what that was going to entail. As Debbie wheeled me out of the room he patted me on the shoulder and said he'd operate as soon as he could.

There was no Fairy Dust this time, but in every other way this second operation was so much better than the horrors of the previous one. Mr. Groom assured me that this time no one would pull me out of bed and try to make me stand as soon as I came round. He offered me the choice of having an epidural (I thought that was only for pregnant ladies) or having my legs paralysed for forty-eight hours to ensure they were pain free while I revived from the operation. I opted for the latter solution and it was very successful. I came round like a bird and lay quietly, feeling nothing at all, while I got myself together and recovered.

So I was ready to face the pain when it came, and the onslaught of the physiotherapists. And the long, grinding hours of exercises that lay ahead.

But this time there was a difference. My new Ilizarov frame was designed to stretch and gently lengthen my leg. There were nuts and bolts on the exterior of every pin through my leg – sixteen in all. I was given a little spanner and instructed that I had to tighten each screw for four turns three times a day. I was lying in bed, but this almost became a full-time job. Once again (as I'd done with the carer's attendance,) I had to draw a grid to make sure I'd do the right number of turns each day. Sometimes the screws were quite hard to twist. The regime continued after I was discharged and back home again. Though at the time it seemed very wearisome – in the end it all paid off. My leg "grew" by a quarter of an inch!

Then, quite suddenly, about three days after the operation, I found myself coughing and wheezing. I couldn't understand it, none of my visitors had had colds or coughs. And it was midsummer. By the time the nurses came on their evening rounds I was struggling to breathe. The Red Indian Sister, who was kind as well as being super-efficient, took my temperature. I didn't need to look at her face. Before I knew it I was on oxygen. I gulped greedily, but even that didn't seem to get down to my lungs. A lot of people came and went and then everything became foggy. I couldn't sleep, I couldn't breathe, and I didn't know what was happening any more. It seemed to be the middle of the night when a strange, rather older, Doctor appeared. I gathered he was a breathing expert, a friend of Mr. Groom's, who'd summoned him. He kept trying to make me breathe into something like a small kettle. I wanted to please him, but I had no breath to go into his little machine. He kept entreating me to try harder, but I was doing all I could. When he finally left he told me to get what sleep I could.

It seemed I'd got pneumonia, something quite likely to happen after a big operation. But with the oxygen, and continually being hooked up to the comforting nebulizer (hot, warm, moist air streams into a mask to help you breathe,) I groped my way back to "normality": turning the screws, and cleaning the frame, and getting out of bed – with assistance. And doing my exercises and hopping, determinedly, on my one good leg and crutches, up and down the corridors.

But a few days later, when I was back in the dreary routine, something very odd happened. Mr. Groom was paying his morning visit and he was standing at the foot of the bed, with the Red Indian Sister, who, although he was Army-officer tall, towered above him. And the rest of his entourage were there, including little wiry Sarah, the physiotherapist. Suddenly, the whole group of them began to recede. They were all growing smaller and smaller, shrinking – in an "Alice In Wonderland" kind of way. Or was it me getting further away from them? What they were all saying no longer concerned me – in fact I couldn't hear their voices any more. I didn't know when they left the room. I wasn't there any longer – I'd finally made my escape. I was far away in some very safe place of my own. Later – or it may have been sooner – I was no longer where time ruled, I was vaguely aware of being transferred from my bed to a stretcher. I was wheeled along corridors and parts of the hospital I never knew existed. I saw other patients, shipwrecked souls in gaping gowns. None of it concerned me any longer.

Finally we reached wherever it was they were taking me. It seemed they wanted to do something to me. I was hoisted onto a high table, where I lay for a long time, but it was timeless.

"Meantime, she chanted snatches of old tunes, as one incapable of her own distress..." My head was full of songs and long forgotten poetry. I wanted to hold it in my mind, remember it forever. Back on the high table, it seemed they couldn't do whatever it was they'd planned. It was all of no concern to me. Their disappointment meant nothing. The dreamlike return journey began. Then, all the golden poetry that I so wanted to hold onto, slipped away as they laid me on my bed again. It seems I slept for twenty-four hours. When I next saw Sarah, the physiotherapist, she asked me what had happened? "You simply weren't here that morning," she said. I couldn't explain – I just smiled wanly. The whole process must have been healing though, especially the long sleep, because after that I really began to get better.

CHAPTER FOUR

2003

Feeling stronger and that at last I was on the road to recovery, my days in hospital passed quickly enough, filled with my one-legged walking and all the other exercises. They, and the tightening of the screws and the daily cleaning of the frame continued after I was delivered home. As usual, by ambulance. Up to now all the crews had been so kind and helpful and full of compassion.

But on this journey home I was unlucky, one of my carriers was a little Indian. He seemed to take an instant dislike to me. (The feeling was mutual.) They always ask your weight, so that they can gauge what they've got to carry. And I realised how difficult it was for them to get me up the fifty stairs to my flat. Usually they made a chair with their hands, which I sat in, with my hands round their necks. On reaching the first landing the little Indian stopped, forcing his friend to do the same. Of course I'd told them my correct weight. Now the nasty little man said accusingly, "You're heavier than that!"

"No, they weighed me at the hospital before I left. That's what I weigh, honest." The Indian pulled an unbelieving face and they stumbled up to the next landing where, obviously by mutual consent, they both dropped me. Very hard. And painfully. "You're too heavy," said the Indian Grouse Leader, wiping a bit of spittle from the side of his mouth. His friend remained silent, staring gloomily at his Nike trainers.

"Well, thank you gentlemen." I gave what I hoped was a Queenly wave from my undignified position on the floor. "I'll make my own way without your valuable assistance." They threw my crutches roughly in my direction, and shuffled away. Out of my life forever, I hoped. Getting up the remainder of the stairs to my front door wasn't difficult, I advanced upwards on my bottom, towing my crutches behind me. The difficulty was getting upright to insert the key in the lock, without falling over backwards and breaking another pin and going back to "go" and certainly spending time, if not in prison, in hospital, which by now to me seemed synonymous. Somehow I managed to hoist myself up on my crutches to a standing position and entered my own flat.

No one ever came to the hospital with me, except the very last time, when I was having the frame removed. Lovely John drove me and waited all day ready to drive me to Denville Hall in the late afternoon. Oh, those monthly visits to the Clinic: waiting and waiting, in the early morning, sitting in my chair ready dressed in my coat and hoping the ambulance would turn up eventually. (It always did, except once, when, with the wrong address, they gave up looking for me.)

Of course, actually being seen by Mr. Groom was the high spot of the day. I soon learnt, once I'd survived the long queue for x-rays, to bag a seat as near to his room as possible. Catching his eye meant you might possibly get seen a little sooner. During the morning he was always sallying out among the patients. He knew everyone's name and had a merry quip for each of us. Once, quite early on, a motorcyclist left his helmet on the seat next to me. Mr. Groom noticed it at once – "Oh, Miss Binns, you've come on your bike? You are making progress!" I laughed for the rest of the day...

One time, after my second operation when I was being looked at, he introduced me to a new machine. Apparently the bones in my leg weren't hardening very well. This machine, if used every day, should speed up the setting process. But it was very expensive. Mr. Groom asked if I could possibly manage to buy one? I swallowed hard and thought of the long time I'd already been recovering, (by then it was almost two years.) I also knew that, eventually, I would get some compensation from Covent Garden. So I agreed to get the thing. And playing it on my leg every morning became another chore after cleaning the pins and before the exercises. I'm sure it did help the hardening process, too. Long after, when I'd finally recovered, I gave it to the hospital. Apparently Mr. Groom was able to recycle them for further use.

At the end of each session with him, he always said, with genuine regret in his voice, "I'm so sorry, I'm going to have to ask you to go for a blood test. It's still not right..."

He knew what horror this entailed. I'd be wheeled down to the Blood Testing area at King's, to be met by the hostile stares of the hundreds of other patients already waiting. My wheelchair pusher would get me a ticket and I'd observe ruefully that I was number 689, and at present they were doing 49. So I'd settle down to the long, boring wait. Coming on crutches and with no companion, it wasn't possible to bring a newspaper or book on my hospital visits. I just had my handbag, with a few necessities, slung round me. Eventually my time to enter the cubicle would come. Usually there was quite a struggle to get the blood, but the needles were nothing and all the nurses highly skilled at this job.

This chore accomplished, I'd be wheeled to the final horror – Transport. If ever there's a parking ground for Lost Souls it's the Transport Department of any big hospital. King's was no exception. It really was, "Abandon All Hope, Ye Who Enter Here." Every face vacant and blank from the tiredness of the long day. And then a faint flickering of hope when a name was called out. "Is it me? Oh, is it me?" I would become completely desperate, shooting my arm up at anything that sounded remotely like "Binns" or was going to West London. All patience lost, I would cajole some passing nurse to wheel me to the Reception Desk. I would brave the Resident Harpies and meekly enquire if there was any sign of anything to take me home. Recklessly I would point out that if I wasn't home by five my carer for the evening would give up and go away. Meaning no supper (and I'd had nothing to eat all day) and no one to help me to bed. The Ladies in Transport remained glassily indifferent to my pleas. It seemed I lived too far away, I wasn't in the King's catchment area. I shouldn't have come to King's in the first place. Why wasn't I attending my local hospital? My ambulances weren't London ones, they came from Kent or the South Coast. I wouldn't have cared if they'd come from the Isle of Wight, (and once they did) if they got me home. And eventually, when I'd resigned myself to spending the rest of my life in Transport, some Angel would appear and actually call my name through the now practically empty hall.

I'd be so exhausted by the day I usually lay down in the ambulance for the journey home. In all the years I was transported to and from King's, I never knew the way. Each ambulance seemed to take a different route. The windows are tiny and it's very difficult to see out. I suppose so that curious passers-by can't see in. But getting nearer home they nearly always went up Park Lane. I would heave myself up and peer through the tiny slot of smoked glass. It became my private ritual to see the Animals' War Memorial, with its inscription "They Had No Choice." At that time I really couldn't make any decisions, I just had to go along with everything from day to day. But each time I passed those sad statues I vowed that I was going to recover and return to a life where I made the choices.

But the life I returned to at the moment was

much as it had been before – the daily battle with the carers – hoping they'd turn up. Frequently they didn't. So I'd have to make urgent phone calls to Social Services, pleading for someone to come and give me a meal. (Interestingly, I, who am very inclined to put on weight, remained the same for three years, despite being completely sedentary!) The meals I did get served were hardly nourishing and so extremely boring. I felt so very helpless and useless and it was only the visits from my wonderful friends that kept me going at all. I so longed to go out and breathe the fresh air. When the ambulance men came each month, I tried to delay them at the front gate so that I could take some deep breaths and gulp the air. Sometimes I wanted to cry out St. Joan's great tirade against her imprisonment: "To shut me from the light of the sky..." I knew the Shaw speech by heart, I'd once done it for an audition. I suspected that I'd spoken it with the emotion of a suburban housewife who's discovered her Waitrose is out of kale. Now, sadly, I knew a bit more about imprisonment and the loss of one's freedom. I knew something of the real emotions needed for Shaw's great speech. I sadly reflected that even nuns and prisoners are allowed short breaks in the fresh air.

Of course there were diversions: unable to do it myself, as I'd always done, I had my hair washed professionally every two or three weeks. I asked Westminster Social Services for the name of a Home Hairdresser who could visit me. The first to come was a little black girl who proved a complete disaster. She assured me she was fully qualified, but I think the course she attended must have been a short weekend one. I dragged the Coronation stool from the hall to the bathroom and positioned it in front of the basin – as I did every morning for my strip-wash. (I so longed to have a bath, quite impossible with the frame of course.) When I was sitting in front of the basin the child attempted to give me a shampoo. She didn't seem to know the difference between hot and cold water and most of the soap was left stickily in my hair. When it came to the setting – I'd mopped most the water off myself and moved to the sitting room, she was unable to cope with the rollers she'd brought with her. She dropped most of them on the floor and when she did manage to twist a wisp of hair, they promptly fell out again. In desperation I held my own hand drier and gave myself a blow-dry. Then I wished her goodbye (and good riddance.)

After that fiasco the Social Services sent Rose and for some years (alas) she became my hairdresser. She was qualified and she never stopped talking about the Salon where she'd been employed for many years, before going freelance. In fact, she never stopped talking at all and I was a captive audience. Maddeningly, she treated me as the most doddering of ancient pensioners. But she was useful, always ready to bring in a bit of shopping or run errands. And she did shampoo my hair quite well, and set it, after her fashion. I tried describing how I wanted my hair. I drew little pictures and diagrams, but it always came out the same. As soon as she'd gone out of the door I brushed the whole thing out, and endeavoured to get it more to my liking. At least it was clean. Rose had a mother who was an excellent seamstress, and who was always willing to do little jobs for me, shortening or taking in or whatever (I always wore long skirts, to cover the frame.) Rose's mother refused any payment, so I would send a discreet £5 note with my grateful thanks.

But it was Rose who, one day, came out with a great truth. Something that was continually on my mind, but not to be spoken aloud. During the entire three years that I was a prisoner in my flat, my brother and his wife, who lived in Wiltshire, came up to visit me only once. Admittedly, for that occasion, they'd prepared an elaborate picnic. "For Gad's sake," declared Rose, "They're your relatives. There are trains – it's not far. Not like they lived the other side of the world. Why don't they come up and see you like once a month?" A question I often asked myself. And there was no answer. Or if there was, it was deeply buried somewhere in the past of my dysfunctional family.

Then there was the Cat Lady. Of course I wanted Mimi, who was still living with Eileen, back with me, even though I wouldn't be able to prepare her food or clean her tray. So I engaged the Cat Lady, who'd once swum The Channel, and came before or after her stint in The Serpentine. For this daily visit she charged me seven guineas. A reduction on her usual fee of eight guineas as I was a long-term client and not a short holiday fill-in. When the time came for me to submit my expenses to Covent Garden, Cat Care was by far the largest bill. Mimi cost much more than my own carers.

Watching helplessly as I did, Cat Caring seemed an easy way to make a living. All the lady did was collect the dirty dish from Mimi's feeding mat beside my chair, stride up to the kitchen and open a packet of cat food, which she'd divide in half. She'd place one portion in a dish and put it in the fridge, and she'd bring the remainder down, together with fresh water, to where my little tabby would be hungrily waiting beside me. As it was usually hours later than she'd expected, Mimi would gulp the food hungrily before disappearing under the bed. She didn't like the Cat Lady – our feelings were mutual.

The dame went back to the kitchen and cleaned Mimi's tray. She waved the bag, containing the soiled contents at me, as she departed for the day. I hoped she put the bag in the dustbin. But after a week or two there were complaints from the other flat owners. It seemed she just chucked the bag haphazardly into the dustbin area. When I confronted her about this she said airily, "Oh, that's all right. I'll throw it over next door's fence..."

But she did get me into one terrible bit of trouble. Being flat-bound, I only heard about it afterwards. It seemed the Cat Lady collided with my eighteen stone carer, Yvonne (Why-vonne) on the house steps. Neither would give way. The Cat Lady claimed she slipped and broke her wrist. She then tried to claim damages from The House saying the steps were covered in moss and were slippery, and therefore dangerous. We had a very unpleasant (and dishonest) agent looking after The House at that time. She blamed me, as, I regret to say, did the other flat holders. The situation was saved when a good friend, coming to visit me, saw the Cat Lady mount her motorbike and drive away with no apparent difficulty, less than two weeks after the incident. So, there was no question of injury or damages, much to my relief.

From time to time the Cat Dame took off on exotic holidays and I would take a deep breath of thankfulness. Her partner, a charming man, replaced her and on his daily visits did anything and everything he could to be helpful. He came early every morning and always offered to make me a most welcome cup of tea while he was cleaning Mimi's tray. He would always ask if I wanted anything brought in the next day. He was a most kind and helpful man. Then the Cat Lady grew jealous of our harmless relationship and she suddenly stopped taking these exotic holidays – South America and Alaska featured, I remember. She made quite sure that I never saw her partner again.

Both times I was in hospital at King's, the Chaplain, who I liked very much, came to visit me often. (I never saw the Chaplain at St. Thomas'. Probably, like the Paperboy, he couldn't make it to the twelfth floor.) But I found the Reverend at King's enormously consoling and cheering. Except on one occasion. I'd had my Times delivered and saw the obituary of the man I'd so wanted to marry. I read the notice and discovered he'd had four marriages. I took it hard that one of them hadn't been me. I was crying quietly when the Chaplain came in. It has always puzzled me that, although I explained, he seemed unable to comprehend my grief and sense of loss. He brought me Communion regularly, which I found both helpful and consoling. When, for the last time, (I was about to be discharged) he asked me if I'd like him to write to my own Vicar, so that I could receive the Eucharist once I was back home. I thanked him and he said he'd arrange it. At that time I'd attended St. Mary Abbots in Kensington (where Beatrix Potter was married) as my Mother had before me, for many years.

So I went home and attempted to get on with my life. The months passed and I heard nothing from St. Mary Abbots. After half a year my brother gave me the Vicar's telephone number. (Yes, he actually did that for me. Now very much the Christian, he took the Church Times.) The Vicar answered my call himself. On hearing my request, he shrugged me off with, "That's the Curate's job" and gave me another telephone number.

So eventually I got to speak to the Curate, a likeable enough middle-aged man. (A late call to the Priesthood, I presumed...) When I mentioned the Chaplain at King's he said, "Oh, yes, I remember. I was going to get round to you –."

"Six months," I ruminated, trying not to be bitter. After that he did bring me Communion sometimes and once even blessed the flat. But soon he passed this duty on to an old Lay Reader, who always stayed for coffee. He had to go up to the kitchen and make the Nescafé for both of us, of course. But once settled, he was rather apt to regale me with the gory details of various stomach operations he'd had. I didn't really look forward to his visits.

But as we approached Christmas, the Curate was still coming. He assured me I would go on the list of the homebound, needing a Christmas Dinner on the Great Day. It would be delivered by a volunteer parishioner. "We do it every year," he said, shaking back his rather over long hair, "For everyone who needs it. And you certainly come into that category."

And so, on this second Christmas Day of my imprisonment, I waited. And waited. But nothing, and no one from the church ever appeared. I was saved from starvation by Eileen's foresight. Before she left for Australia, she'd popped into Marks and Spencer's and brought me a little plastic tray with a slice of something described as turkey, two Brussel sprouts and a potato. And wonder of wonders, a Carer turned up mid-afternoon and was able to warm this feast in the oven for me. And that was Christmas, that was.

Eileen, when she returned from Australia, was so distressed about my missed Christmases that she was determined to make it up to me. Much later, when I'd very nearly recovered, she invited me over for lunch at her house in Fulham. I was able to take a taxi then, it was the first time in three years. I still couldn't walk very well and needed two sticks, but at least I was able to get down the stairs. It was a hot July day and Sue opened the front door. I was surprised that all the curtains were drawn, but there were more surprises to come. Eileen embraced me and led me straight into the dining room. The room was candlelit and there were carols playing on the radiogram. And there was a Christmas dinner all laid out – the table was decorated with Poinsettias (where had Sue found them in midsummer?) and ivy and there were crackers beside every place. There were little dishes of nuts and preserved ginger and every other Christmas sweetmeat. I gasped with pleasure, and then I think I cried a bit. It wasn't just the two Christmases I'd missed, it was all the other Christmases rolled into one.

Eileen and Sue disappeared to the kitchen and soon returned bringing the fat turkey and a steaming ham, all the vegetables and all the trimmings and of course we had a flaming pudding. I had a bit of everything – I hadn't eaten so much for years. Eileen sat at the head of the table, beaming with pleasure as I finished every morsel.

After our Dickensian feast we were too full to do anything but loll about on the sofa. We watched a repeat of "Eastenders," (Sue and Eileen were keen followers – I'm a "Corrie" fan myself.) And then it was time for the ordered taxi to take me home. Feeling happier than I'd been for so long, I was never able to thank Eileen properly for that wonderful day. Or really explain just how much it meant to me.

When Eileen died suddenly of a stroke, in 2008, a light went out of my life. She was one year older than me, but when we went out together she described me as "her little sister." But she'd been the mother I never really had. Although she had a big family of her own, she'd found room to include me. So through her I learnt something of being in a normal family – something I'd never had before. And, leaving me with this enormous debt of gratitude, but also the grievous wound of loss.

I first met Eileen when my mother and I knocked on her door, in search of a kitten. Our old cat had had to be put to sleep and my mother demanded an instant replacement. I was busy doing a "Z Cars" and begged her to wait. But no, she had to have a kitten – now. Which was why, after I'd made several telephone calls, we ended up on Eileen's doorstep. And yes, she had one kitten left, from a litter her son had landed on her. So she gave us Mimi and we kept in touch. But it was after the death of her husband Bert, and I had the accident, that she really came into my life. Now I miss her every day.

CHAPTER FIVE

1931

On the Christmas Day I spent so miserably alone, eating the Marks and Spencer meal Eileen had bought for me, I thought of all the other Christmases of my life. Being a child in the Close at Lichfield, hanging up Grandpa's thick golf stockings. (He was past playing all the years I knew him – limping from a hip he'd put out doing the high-jump at Marlborough. In those days they didn't know enough to put it back.) Father Christmas obligingly filled these with an orange and a few simple toys. A model horse, if I was lucky. Morning service in the Cathedral, listening to the King's speech on the wireless in Grandpa's study and playing "Murder" in the evening. During the war the house was filled with evacuees, the army officers were the most congenial. One of these, Colonel Evans, remained a staunch friend to me and Marje long after the war was over.

Peter and I used to put on plays in the drawing room, the alcove there formed a natural stage. Colonel Evans often helped us with these. Once, I believe, he told his astonished staff they must get on with the war without him, he had a play to stage-manage.

I wondered what Christmases were like in the

Close before I was born. I popped into the world on a January evening just as the Cathedral clock was striking nine. I was handed straight into the ready-starched arms of the Monthly Nurse and not returned to my mother until the regulated feeding hour. In those days the great Dr. Spock ruled the nurseries, so I was not picked up when I cried, but left in my pram to howl the hours away in the wintry garden. Until I gave myself a hernia. Then things changed for the better. My Grandfather, who I always regarded as the last of the Victorians, couldn't bear my solitary crying and often limped down to the garden to give me a cuddle, I'm sure a comfort to both of us.

With a penny strapped to my tummy for my hernia, I grew and flourished. Peter and Permanent Nanny, who'd been evacuated for my birth, returned. Peter, two years older than me, was the darling of Nanny's eyes, until, at a very early age, he was sent away to school, then she transferred her affections to me.

My father, Punch – an Army Officer – left for India three weeks after my birth. After three years he returned for a brief visit. Peter and I were attendants at his sister's wedding. I revelled in my pretty white dress with a blue sash and was thrilled when we were taken to a large toy shop and told to choose a present. The toy dog on wheels I selected was my constant companion for the next few years. Marje, my mother, was offered the chance to go out to India to be with my father. She refused and despite having a permanent Nanny, cited "the children" as her excuse!

I was nearly seven when my father returned. Everything suddenly changed – we started life as an Army family. It was a shock after the quiet years in the Close with Granny and Grandpa. My father's regiment – the East Yorks – was posted to Farnborough and Peter and I were to attend a nearby day school. Peter was an old hand but school was a whole new experience for me. On the appointed day, my mother, Marje, put me on a child's bike and gave me a push. Nanny and Peter, accomplished cyclists, steamed ahead. At the school gates I fell off. For that first horrifying day I was allowed to sit with Peter in his class. Everything passed over my head, I hadn't a clue what was going on. At break time, Peter mysteriously disappeared. I walked the gravel paths of the garden alone. I had an urge to pee, but was too shy to ask for the loos. A big girl, passing, pointed an accusing finger at the puddle. "It's been raining," I muttered and wished I was dead.

But things got better, as they do. My father was transferred to Crownhill, then a small village outside Plymouth. I attended a little school for the Officers' children – God forbid we should mix with other ranks! But at last my education really began. Peter had been sent back to the Farnborough school as a boarder. His appendix burst, and he was only saved by the kindly matron who summoned a doctor just in time. Nanny told me Peter was going to die and I couldn't help feeling pleased.

So Peter came home pale, weak and sickly and had to be pushed everywhere on Marje's bike. I seized my chance and moved in as "Daddy's Girl." I stood proudly beside him when he took the salute after Sunday services and pretended not to mind the gunfire when we watched manoeuvres. Peter was already showing talent as a pianist and especially when we were at Lichfield, was shown off to visitors like the infant Mozart. I was securely shut behind the closed nursery doors.

Meanwhile, Mummy and Nanny were getting thick as thieves. They wore identical clothes, bought from catalogues, and huddled over the smelly Valor stove on which our meals were cooked. Punch seemed to spend less and less time in the house and Marje started to cry a lot. I often heard her sobbing in the loo and mostly she forgot to lock the door.

Every school holidays Peter and I were sent back to Lichfield where Granny and Grandpa welcomed us warmly. Granny was a very special person. She'd been a great tennis player in her youth. As Helen Jackson, she'd won the Scots, Welsh and North of England tournaments and also Buxton. Her career culminated at Wimbledon in 1895, where she was runner-up in the Women's Finals. But that year she also won the Mixed Doubles and the Women's Doubles. But she put all her triumphs behind her after her marriage to my Grandfather. I didn't know anything at all about her career until after her death in 1940. All her tennis trophies were destroyed by a fire at her home,

Bellister Castle in Northumberland in 1901. In 1976, cousin Faith gave Bellister to the National Trust.

Being at Lichfield was lovely for Peter and me, with our indulgent grandparents and a large garden to explore and play in. The house was a Grace and Favour residence, it's now the Bishop's Palace. My Grandfather was the Bishop's legal secretary and Diocesan Registrar. After the Easter holidays, 1939, Peter went back to his Preparatory School (he was subsequently expelled.) I remained at Lichfield and Nanny was supposed to give me lessons, but didn't. She wasn't the cuddly Nan of storybooks, but a fierce gypsyish woman with a flaring temper. A doctor who looked after me in later life described her as "a half-educated peasant."

On September 3rd I was walking with her by the Minster Pool and the Cathedral Clock struck eleven. Nanny said, "We are at war." A few weeks later I started in the Junior School of the local Grammar, The Friary. Granny was spending more and more time in her room – the following year she died of bowel cancer. I wasn't allowed to go to her funeral, in those days children didn't have emotions. I was sent to stay with a mean little girl in the big house on the hill, who had her own pony. I was completely devastated. I'd loved Granny more than anyone else in the world. Before her death, she'd done me a special good turn – she'd sacked Nanny. She was the only one strong enough to do this. Nanny had always resented this tiny little person – Gran was only 4'10", but she had a will of iron. So, cursing and weeping by turns, Nanny left the Close forever.

I'd always slept in the nursery at Lichfield – a big airy room with a balcony (forbidden to us children) that overlooked the garden. One night when I was undressing, Marje came in and sat on the bed. She told me Punch was going to marry someone else and I'd never see him again. I could hardly take this in, coming as it did so soon after Granny's death. This was going to be a messy business – divorce was practically unheard of in those days – except for wicked Mrs. Wallis and Edward, "The man born to be King." It finished any confidence Marje had ever had. Being the innocent party, she had to go up to Court in London to give evidence, and it nearly killed her. I waved her off – she was wearing a green wool suit. My Grandfather, a legal man himself, spent a fortune he didn't have trying to get my father to pay maintenance, but slippery Punch always managed to duck the Court Orders.

Once the divorce proceedings were over, Marje immersed herself in War Work at the local Forces canteen. I was desolate and completely heartbroken. Marje and I had never bonded since the time when, with a girlish giggle, she told me she'd tried everything she could think of to abort me, when she found she was pregnant for the second time. Apparently she'd taken boiling hot baths, drunk gin by the gallon and even practiced jumping off the kitchen table. But to her annoyance, none of these activities had budged me. I'd clung on for what was, indeed, dear life. Punch had left and my beloved Granny had gone. When I was free from schoolwork, I wandered alone about the large deserted house. I was desperate for something to love. At mealtimes in the dark red-papered dining room, tears would sometimes pour down my cheeks. My Grandfather would say, "I think you'd better go to your room." Of course childhood depression was quite unheard of then.

And suddenly my Godmother, Maude Fanshawe, became a Fairy one. She sent me a cheque for £15, apparently for missed Christmases and Birthdays. Without any hesitation, I announced I was going to buy a pony. (I'd been devouring pony books and Gran had arranged for me to have some riding lessons on the local milk pony, Tommy.)

Looking back it seems fairly unbelievable that I managed this, virtually alone, at ten years old. But I was desperate. I bought a pony. Through my school friend, Mary, I heard of a little Welsh roan pony mare for sale. She was unbroken. One Saturday afternoon I persuaded Grandpa to drive me out to this farm. (He got extra petrol coupons for his bad leg.) I bought her for £10. I'd found a field, not far from the Close, where she could be turned out – for 2/6 a week. Just my pocket money at the time. I bought a second hand bridle and a felt saddle for £4 and a dandy brush and a bucket with the remaining £1. I was undeterred that Pippin, as I christened her, was unbroken. Using methods that wouldn't have disgraced Monty Roberts, I gradually tamed her. She never really got used to traffic, on busy roads I used to dismount and lead her.

Halcyon days followed, as I groomed her, tended her and cared for her. I joined a local Pony Club, went to a few gymkhanas and rode her all over Staffordshire whenever my schoolwork permitted.

Before the arrival of Pippin, I'd always been a Munchkin, far too short for my age. But with the happiness of having my own pony to love, I began to grow. Soon my legs were dangling far below Pippin's belly (I often rode her bareback.) My lovely Grandpa stepped in and said he would buy me a bigger pony. (He was so pleased I showed an aptitude for riding. Neither Peter nor I could hit a ball in any sport. We'd not inherited any of Granny's talent.) He was as good as his word and also agreed that Pippin could be kept. He selected a Show Pony from an ad on the front page of The Times. I was nearly sick with excitement as I watched the beautiful bay kicking and bucking her way down the ramp of the horse box that had brought her from Tring. Riding Gypsy was terrifying at first. She tried every trick from bolting to bucking me off. I persevered with love, patience and titbits and suddenly everything changed and we were friends for life. But she remained hugely temperamental. Once we were expelled from the ring at a show, the judge decreeing, "She wasn't a suitable pony for a child to ride."

When I was sixteen my mother took me to Scotland for a week's holiday. The day after our return, there was a horse show at Rugeley. Gypsy hadn't been exercised and was on heat and highly excited. She danced on her toes throughout the long ride to the show. I should have been warned. Or should someone have warned me? She crashed and bashed through every fence in the Junior Jumping. But we were winning the Obstacle Race – I'd vaulted on and was half across the saddle when Gypsy saw something in the crowd and shied violently. I hit the ground with a sickening thud, my right leg was twisted beneath me. I looked up at the red ball that was the setting sun and realised I'd often dreamt of that moment. And I knew I'd never go back to school.

At about the time I got Pippin, my mother became happier, too. She was having an affair with the Bishop (only the suffragan.) I should have been glad for her, but at the time I was slightly resentful. Mrs. Bishop was still alive and she'd always been kind to me. For Peter, Marje's affair was a lifesaver – when he was expelled from his public school, the Bishop pleaded his case, saying my brother's behaviour was entirely due to the upset of the divorce! The Bishop arranged for him to go to the day school in Lichfield, and to my chagrin, he came down to The Friary for "extra biology." Peter always had an eye for girls and was soon inveigling some of my fellow pupils back to the Close, where, in the attic, he had a laboratory, among other things. I nearly died of embarrassment when the Head Girl told me not to run up the stairs, knowing my brother had shagged her the previous afternoon.

It was meant to be a great secret, but we'd known about Marje's affair for months. Then my

Grandfather suddenly found out. He was devastated – the Bishop was his best friend (he left him the billiard table in his will.) On discovering the shameful news, his first edict was, "The child (me) must go to boarding school!" To blame me for Marje's misconduct seemed terribly unfair. I'd been talking myself out of the boarding school threat for several years, pointing out I'd won a scholarship to The Friary, etc. But Gramp was adamant and stuck to his word. His criterion was that the school must be as far away from Lichfield as possible. He selected one from the ads in The Times (just as he'd found Gypsy.) I was entered for an Institution for the education of young ladies at Folkestone. During the summer my mother went to London and interviewed the Headmistresses, but when I went in September it was being run by two quite different dames. I was taking my School Certificate and everyone, including the new school, told me I would fail. It was all arranged that I would go into the Upper V and take it again. So, when my results came and I'd done rather well, with distinctions in English, etc, I thought I might just scrape a reprieve. But no, in September I was packed off to join the VIth form on the South Coast.

To say I was miserable at Brampton Down is an understatement. Suicidal is nearer the mark. I missed my ponies and all the other animals quite dreadfully and found the togetherness of boarding school stifling. Grandpa had agreed that the ponies would be kept on for me in the holidays, and with a slight softening of heart, arranged for me to have riding lessons in the summer term. This extra-curricular break gave me the one moment of magic during my entire time at Folkestone. One summer's afternoon, the man who was taking the ride ordered us to rein in our rather sad ponies beneath an oak tree: "Listen!" he said, and for the first and only time in my life I heard a nightingale sing. A never-to-be-forgotten experience.

Another reason for my unhappiness was the vast amount of free time I had. As far as I could see, the only purpose for being there was to learn as much as I could. But with my unexpected arrival in the tiny VIth form, there weren't enough mistresses to give me extra subjects. I had "elocution" lessons with a very sympathetic teacher. These weren't about learning to speak beautifully but in-depth study and learning by heart of wonderful poems (I won several prizes for the school, reciting at local festivals.) This lovely lady sensed my unhappiness and I believe even wrote to Lichfield suggesting that it would be wise to remove me from the school. Our weekly letters home were censored, but I'd discovered a secret pillar box, where, by hiding missives under my brown felt hat, I could send appeals home without interference. Every morning, I strolled to the cliff top and back. At least I was senior enough to escape the run round the block before breakfast, obligatory for the rest of the boarders.

But the summer holidays came at last and I was back with my ponies. As I've described, Marje took me to Scotland for a short holiday. And then it was the Rugeley Horse Show. I sang, "Oh What A Beautiful Morning" to Gypsy as she danced her way towards the event that was going to change my life forever.

CHAPTER SIX

1949

It took four operations and the insertion of a plate to set my leg after the riding accident. This was followed by a year in plaster. But at last I was ready to start learning to walk again. There was no physiotherapy in those days, a lady came with a bucket of water. I put my foot in the bucket and she gave me some electric shocks. That was it. I announced that I wanted to go on the stage. I was walking now, but with a very pronounced limp. So my Grandfather agreed to this — to him an outrageous proposal, but privately he thought by being an actress I would manage to cure myself. Which I did, but unfortunately in my ignorance I was using all the wrong muscles, and a few years later I really ran into trouble, until I was saved by the wonderful Alexander Technique. Later, I had the great privilege of lessons with Irene Tasker, doyenne of the movement, and Alexander's long-serving secretary.

I began by writing to all the major drama schools, and received much the same reply from all of them. At that time all their places and scholarships were reserved for the men and women coming out of the forces. Unless, of course, you possessed real star quality, which I most certainly didn't. They all suggested I should contact them again in three or four years.

But I was anxious to begin my life, so I walked down to the local Repertory Company, who performed in the David Garrick Theatre, which was really a converted cinema. Much to my surprise I was taken on as an A.S.M. (Assistant Stage Manager) at £2 per week. And this at a time when would-be actors were paying premiums of £100 or £200 just for the chance to get into such a company. The old manager who engaged me – he seemed to have no neck at all, and resembled an ancient tortoise, told me he would make me a provisional member of Equity straight away. At the time I didn't realise how important this was. Later, in my second job which was with a non-Equity company, I realised my luck. At this time, before Margaret Thatcher busted the Unions, it was extremely hard to get your Equity card. Many later well-known actresses only got their full membership by working in nightclubs and other such dives to serve their 40 weeks apprenticeship.

So I started work, and was full of enthusiasm for all the menial tasks that came my way – sweeping the stage, making tea for all the company and going round the dressing room doors before the evening performance. The only blot on my technicoloured landscape was the director, Kenneth Tynan. Later to become so famous, or rather notorious, he summed me up in an instant. As a shy country-bumpkin teenager, I was fair game for his teasing, which was merciless. He was straight out of Oxford and sporting his purple suits, which hung loosely on his almost skeletal body. My heart sank when he sent for me, which he did almost every day. He'd be lounging in the Prop Room, the inevitable cigarette hanging from his lower lip. His favourite ploy was to send me to telephone his current lady-loves in London, making rendezvous for the weekend (he always made his get-away from the dull provincial city.) As he was having a blazing affair with the leading lady at Lichfield, he knew having to do this embarrassed me hugely. Later, he let this highly-talented actress down with a bang, and ruined her promising career.

Ken did give me my first part – as an ugly lady-in-waiting in Garrick's strange version of "The Taming of the Shrew." I was upset at not getting the Princess, the part went to the other vastly attractive and decidedly nubile A.S.M. who left at the same time as Tynan. Still, I was "on the boards," and my life as an actress had begun. The production gave me another life-changing moment. Ken had chosen the overture to "The Marriage of Figaro" for the play. As well as acting my little part, it was my duty to play the records on the panatrope. I listened entranced. At home with my brother, a would-be organist, I had heard nothing but Church music. Mozart came to me as a revelation, to be investigated further, and later still, a life-long passion.

Ken was replaced by Geoffrey Wardwell – a middle aged Teddy Bear of a man. My life became easier, and I was thrilled when Geoffrey took me on one side and told me to understudy Cinderella for the forthcoming pantomime. I immediately learnt the lines, and took every opportunity I could snatch to watch the juvenile lead, Elizabeth James, who I liked and admired, at work. Tynan had had a policy of bringing well-known actors up for "special" productions, and this was continued. There was a well-known character actor – I think it was in "The Enchanted Cottage." (I gave my all as a non-speaking Victorian ghost on the stairs.) The poor man was dreadfully unsure of his lines, so I was placed behind the fireplace as an extra prompt. Unfortunately I couldn't see the actor – he seemed to me to be pausing all the time, so I kept feeding him lines. Too keen – still a fault – the hapless actor had no option but to tell the fireplace to "Shut up!"

Lionel Jeffries came up for a production. Many years later I read in his autobiography, "What a thrill it had been to tread the actual boards used by Garrick." As the theatre was a converted cinema, it seemed his imagination had been running into overtime.

Christmas came, and I'd watched Elizabeth James give her lovely performance as Cinderella at the dress rehearsal. We were having our traditional Christmas lunch at my Grandfather's house in the Close when the telephone rang. It was Mrs. Cowlishaw, who ran the theatre with her son Anthony. She told me that Elizabeth James had had a car accident, and I would be opening the next day. After making sure that Elizabeth was not badly injured, I proceeded with the utmost calm. I assured my employer that I'd just finish my lunch, and then get down to the theatre to rehearse and try the cozzies. I was so new in the theatre that it never occurred to me to be nervous. I'd read all the theatre books, and this was what happened. The understudy gets her chance, and takes over... Now, after a lifetime in the business, I'd be so nervous I really doubt I'd get on at all! Then, it seemed the most natural thing in the world, and I proceeded accordingly.

The Principal Boy was marvellous, and undoubtedly "carried me" particularly in the songs, which I'm afraid I left to her entirely. (Like Mark Twain, "As a singist I have never been a success.") I hopped about during the dances, and spouted my lines like a trouper. There can't have been much hard news about that weekend, because all the local papers came. There's nothing like 'local girl makes good', especially at Christmas. I got glowing reviews. What is laughingly known as 'my career' has been downhill ever since.

Luckily Elizabeth James recovered quickly enough to resume playing Cinderella for the second week. I went back to my lowly duties in the prompt corner. But I'd had my chance and, I hope, taken it. I had a few more little acting parts, but as summer approached I grew restless. Two new female A.S.M.'s had joined the company, and I saw my chances of getting parts diminishing. So I gave in my notice. Everyone, from the old manager to the newest A.S.M. told me I was mad. I knew I was –

but I wanted to act. Within three weeks, without leaving Lichfield, I'd got a job as the juvenile lead with a company at Newcastle-under-Lyme. I'd answered an advert in "The Stage," and the whole thing was done by letter (and photo.) They wanted someone small, as Gerald Hughes, who ran the company with his wife, was pretty short. I went up to Macclesfield, and lived in a caravan for the first and only time in my life. I shared this accommodation with the other young girls. We were only there for the week's rehearsal. Then we moved to Newcastle-under-Lyme, where we played in the Town Hall. As it was Newcastle in Staffordshire I was near enough to Lichfield to be able to go home at weekends. I was able to raid the dressing-up box and search around for clothes for the next week's production. We did quite a number of period plays – I did the leading girl in two old Ivor Novellos – "The Rat" and "I Lived With You." I played Isabella Linton in "Wuthering Heights" – my part, I was never a Cathy! But that was my first brush with dramatisations of the Brontës' work. Many more were to follow in the coming years.

I found digs with a lovely family. The father worked in the famous Wedgwood factory – and one afternoon he took me on a tour of the fascinating pottery. They had two schoolgirl daughters, and the wife was so kind to me. The original arrangement was that I paid two guineas a week, just for my (very nice) room and breakfast. But soon this lovely lady was saying, "I've left some pie and peas in the oven for you. Don't bother to bring anything in. I cooked plenty for all of us..." So before very long I was having full board with this friendly couple. At least I was able to bring them fruit and veg from the garden at Lichfield when I returned to work early on Mondays.

I was earning £4/10s a week – the Equity minimum wage at the time. Looking back – there's never been a time when I've felt so rich! Newcastle market provided many delights, I stocked up my wardrobe for years to come with dresses at £1 each. We went to the cinema frequently in the afternoons, and being Equity members we got in for free. Heaven knows when we found time to learn our lines, we were a repertory company doing a fresh play every week. But the Hughes, who ran the company, had been doing the same plays for aeons. The character man and Maisie the character lady had been with them for years, too. So the rehearsals centred on us, the younger ones. Some of the productions had been going so long that we didn't even have proper scripts. We were handed what are called "sides," pieces of card with your lines on them, but nothing else except your actual cues. This often led to some confusion as it was difficult to make out the plot and what the play was really about. But we muddled through. As you always do in Rep. All the other young people were friendly and supportive, though the Hughes, of course, were rather distant. We never saw them, except at rehearsals, and Gerald in the play at night. Mrs. Hughes never came in in the evenings.

I think all the trouble started when we did

"The Bells." Yes, we actually played it, though now I'm so old I've stopped mentioning it, as most people seem to have as vague a sense of time as I have, and automatically assume I did this old melodrama with Henry Irving! (It was one of the great Victorian actor's showpieces. He put it on whenever business was bad. It still is a great crowd-puller.) But no, it was with Gerald Hughes I did it, and as the maidservant I had the immortal line, "It's the bells, Burgomaster! I can hear the bells!" So Gerald was going full throttle and exacting every ounce of drama from this old piece. I think he got above himself. It was that week, when we kissed on stage, he started putting his tongue into my mouth. I was so young and innocent I thought this must be part of being a proper actress. After all, he was my employer... So, mindful of how difficult it was to get jobs in the theatre (even then) I said nothing and carried on. But for me the writing was on the wall. Mrs. Hughes, fat and resentful that she could no longer play the ingénues opposite her husband, smelt trouble. Gerald's behaviour towards me grew worse. And then all the affectionate petting stopped abruptly. Mrs. Hughes gave me my notice – her excuse being, "My voice was too weak."

Of course I was devastated, and my confidence shattered. To get the sack from my second job! It didn't bear thinking about. I said 'goodbye' to my lovely family in the Potteries, and with my tail between my legs I took the bus back to Lichfield. My dear Grandfather had given me the fare home. He continued to do this for his few remaining years. Usually a ten shilling note (those were the days.) He told me to put it into my Post Office Savings Book, only to be used in emergencies. He said I was always to remember the house in the Close was my home. (Though it wasn't going to be for much longer.)

I didn't stay dispirited for long. Once back in Lichfield I took "The Stage" and busily answered adverts. And for Christmas I got another job, once again from a letter. I was going to be Second Girl in a touring pantomime – somewhere up north. That we were to do three performances a day, including Christmas Day itself, did not deter me or quench my enthusiasm. I was a working actress. This is what real actresses did. At that young age it didn't occur to me that I'd be better off being out-of-work in London and working at Lyons Corner House.

I set off for the shabby theatre in a Manchester suburb where we were to have the three days rehearsal and play for the first week. As a lowly member of the company I discovered my dressing room – at the very top of the antiquated building, up many flights of stone stairs. There was a washbasin, with running cold water. I was to learn this was a luxury, in many of the theatres we played on that tour there was a bucket used for everything, by everybody, in the dressing room. Above this basin was a fixed notice. "Kindly Do Not Stand In the Basin. Severe Lacerations Have Resulted."

I'd learnt my lines, of course, from the much-thumbed typed script that had arrived in the post. As Polly Garter I had my favourite stage direction of

all time – "Exit, laughing as if not caring." A good maxim to get through life as a jobbing actress. When they discovered I could speak and read, they gave me practically all the dialogue in the entire show. All the plot, that is. I quickly learnt that comedians and speciality acts (we had "The Great Norris and his Performing Pigeons") will give away nothing in rehearsal. They take centre stage, mumble something no one can hear, and say, "Joke over." Great, if you're waiting for a cue to come on…
As always, I'd been perfectly honest about my non-singing abilities. So I was a bit nonplussed to discover I was to help the principal comedian with the Community Song. I needn't have worried. Of all the company this man was the most resentful of me. Understandably, I expect I did come over as rather "posh" in those far-away days. As soon as the song sheet for "I taught I taw a puddy-cat" was lowered into place, he practically edged me off the stage. There was no question of me opening my mouth. This was His Song and I was just about allowed to point to the words with a stick as the audience lustily joined in. There were four bigger, busty girls, who, as villagers, formed the chorus. We all shared a dressing room, so I got to know them well. Their one idea was to get a job in a hairdressers once the panto ended. They couldn't understand why I should possibly want to make a career on the stage – such a thing was utterly beyond their comprehension. But it was the juvenile troupe – "The Manchester Mites," that got my attention. I watched these tiny girls, blue with cold, huddling

together in the wings. On tour, as well as their board and keep, they got half-a-crown a week, which went directly back to their mums, badly needing this minute sum after paying for the dancing lessons that had got them into the troupe. It was difficult to get The Mites to say anything, but one told me that on the tour they all slept in the same bed. "But it keeps us warm, Miss," she added.

This kind of tatty three-shows-a-day panto was one of the things that disappeared when television sets became generally available. Remembering "The Manchester Mites," I can't help thinking this was a good thing. The Great British Public began demanding, and expecting, higher standards in their entertainment. Though looking at the offerings on television nowadays, I do wonder if entertainment has advanced very much.

On this tour I gained my first real experience of theatrical digs. It wasn't a very happy learning curve (as they say.) The story of the landlady, who, when an actor brings in a bunch of asparagus hoping it will be cooked for his supper, later gets the reply, "I put your bluebells in water," isn't far from the truth. For me, the greatest embarrassment was going through the kitchen, the eyes of the whole family upon you, to ask for your square of newspaper before visiting the loo up the garden. Lucky male performers – there were nearly always potted plants in the house.

We played Barrow-in-Furness, and my mother decided she'd come up and visit me. When she arrived at my digs I was already at the theatre, doing the first show of the day. My landlady showed her my room. My mother was horrified to find a man in the bed. He greeted her calmly enough, "Tis my bed by day, your daughter 'as it o'nights." My mother went off to see the circus, also playing in the town. As far as I remember, I didn't even change my digs after this incident. I was busy being a real actress.

The following year I was back in a similar pantomime. Only this time I was in "Dick Whittington." I'd answered yet another advert in "The Stage", this time for "Cat, own skin...", which clearly I hadn't got, so when I heard, by letter, I'd got the job, I had to hire one from London. This cost one pound ten shillings a week. My wages were six pounds ten, so there wasn't much left over to live on. When I unpacked it at the theatre I really felt I'd been swindled – it was more like a great shaggy dog than a cat. It had probably been a skin for Nana in some sixth rate tour of "Peter Pan."

I cannot imagine how I had the conceit to imagine I could play a Cat. All the pantomime animals – Mother Goose, Dick Whittington's friend, even the Horse, require years of professional dedication and training. The artistes who play them are specialists in their own rights. I was a rank outsider and an amateur trying to imitate their skills, which I clearly hadn't got. On arrival at the theatre – we were in Wales this time, the management told me the Cat traditionally walks round the rim of the dress circle. Untrained as I was, I refused point blank, and blotted my copybook for the rest of the tour. As well as worrying about my own safety, I feared for the audience who would be seated below. My "speciality" act was equally pathetic – I played with a mock fishbone I'd made from a wire coat hanger, as I lumbered about the stage in this great thick heavy skin. From the first show onwards, and we were again doing three a day, it never dried out. Of course there was no heating in the theatre, so when I came to put it on the next day, it was still sopping wet. Inevitably I caught a cold. Which soon became what I supposed was bronchitis, as I was finding it difficult to breathe. The days passed, and I lumbered more and more slowly about the stage. There were of course no understudies. There was no question of being off, or of missing any of each day's three performances.

I had made friends with the girl who played the Fairy. (Her speciality act included playing the accordion.) I honestly think Beverley saved my life. She'd given up the struggle with digs, and for the final week of the panto – we were playing Llandudno – she was renting a beach hut. By then I was feeling so ill I didn't need much persuasion to join her. So every night after the final show we staggered along the shingle. But once inside the hut I was warmer than I'd been for the whole tour. Beverley tucked me up in the top bunk, and made me a hot drink. I think it was laced with something stronger, because I soon fell into a wakeful sleep. I half woke many times, and it was wonderful to be in the warm hut, heated by a Primus stove, and hear the waves crashing against the shingle outside.

The next day, until it was time to go to the theatre for the first show, my Good Fairy kept me wrapped up and warm, and fed me slices of orange – all I was able to swallow. She told me stories of the months she'd spent in Ireland with her boyfriend, Malachy, and how he'd taught her the few chords she could play on the accordion. Which had led to her job in "Dick Whittington." She confided to me how she hoped to go to Italy to study to become a real singer. I thought she had a beautiful voice, and always listened to her solo number. We remained friends, and met up again in London. A few years later she realised her dream, and went out to Rome to have her voice trained. It was a hard life, she kept herself by giving English lessons, but it took grit to persevere as she did. She appeared in several Italian films, including Fellini's "8½." And she invited me out to stay, so I had a number of holidays in the Eternal City. Picnicking in the Tuscan hills, the graves in those days were just ruins among the long grass. (I met a snake, and Beverley was bitterly jealous) and bathing far down the coast below Rome, (Beverley had a little Fiat, which she drove intrepidly through the traffic jams.) These were among the happiest days of my life. She even got me an interview with Fellini. I was seen by a henchman first, but I heard the Great Man in the next room – the door was open – ask what I was like? For the first and last time I was described as "Molto Bella." But tragedy was lying in wait. I rejoiced when Beverley married a young Italian, but within months of the wedding she died of cancer.

CHAPTER SEVEN

1953

A dark tunnel was also starting in my life. As the pantomime was finishing I received a telegram from my mother saying I must return home immediately. My Grandfather had dementia and was dying. The first problem was the trains. In those days none ran on Sundays in Wales, so my journey to Lichfield had to be postponed until the following day. It gave me a chance to recover a bit, and prepare myself for what was to come. Beverley and I had a last day together by the sea.

My Grandfather didn't die for another six weeks. The doctor insisted we kept feeding him. I've wondered why, ever since? I was the only person who could get him to take anything, so I sat miserably at his bedside, watching him suffering, and trying to get him to take sips of slops of bread and milk. He didn't know who I was, and confused the act of taking nourishment with spitting. So when at last his death came, it was a great relief.

We had no money. Grandpa gave Marje, my mother, a small allowance. She'd used all that in caring for him the last couple of months. With the cat skin costing so much, and paying for digs, all my small earnings had gone as well. Marje gave me a cheque on my Grandfather's account and told me to go to the bank and cash it. I was met with a blank refusal. My Grandfather was dead. The account of J. Murray Atkins was closed. We were desperate – there were the funeral costs to pay. And before my Grandpa's body was cold, one of the Canons of the Close burst in and informed us that we'd have to quit the Grace and Favour house in four weeks! (My Grandfather had lived there for twenty-nine years.) So much for Christian charity. I had a brainwave, I searched the front page of The Times – in those days crammed with interesting adverts. I selected, and contacted, one Mr. Spink, who was interested in buying fine paintings. I knew the two pictures in the dining room, though unsigned, were reputed to be by Zuccarelli. Mr. Spink couldn't get them into his car quickly enough. Dizzy with our success, Marje and I threw in an Old Crome of Norwich that was languishing on the stairs. Mr. Spink gave us a cheque for the princely sum of £100. In those days worth quite a bit, but still... However, it got us out of a hole and kept us going as we toiled day and night to clear the accumulation that filled the thirty-six rooms of the house in the Close. It's now the Bishop's Palace.

We had a two day sale in the house of everything that remained after Mr. Spink's clearance, which did quite well. Lovely Peter Stockham thought I'd find it very painful, and kindly took me to Birmingham the first day. But I was past minding and quite interested in seeing how much things fetched.

We packed up our few personal belongings, and prepared to start a new life, with no idea where that was going to be. Marje set off on a series of visits, and I went to stay with my Grandfather's sister at her house in Rickmansworth. My one idea was to get back to acting, and Aunt Gladys's house was within easy commuting distance of London. Sadly I'd missed the chance to be a Woman of Canterbury in the production of "Murder in the Cathedral," at the Old Vic during Grandpa's illness. Once again I started writing job letters. Fairly quickly, through some connection of the missed T.S. Eliot play, I got an audition for one that was going to be put on in Westminster Abbey. I went to meet the director, Hugh Green, actually in the Abbey, and did my carefully prepared speech for him. It was a disaster. Ever since Grandpa's death I'd noticed croakiness and irritation in my throat. Now my voice had virtually disappeared. Hugh could not have been nicer, or handled the situation more tactfully. He knew all about "Your trumpets, Angels," the play I'd been in for the Festival of Britain in Southwark Cathedral, and said he would certainly have given me a part, but with my voice as it was, employing me was quite out of the question. He urged me to seek vocal help, and said he'd have a word with Clifford Turner, the renowned teacher at RADA, who was a friend of his.

Clifford... who usually only taught the men, agreed to take me on privately, and for some months I went up for weekly lessons in one of the

Central School's rooms at Hyde Park Gate. Slowly and patiently Clifford helped me to rebuild my voice. After the shock of Grandpa's death, and suddenly finding myself in charge of everything, it seemed I'd had a kind of vocal breakdown, instead of a nervous one. Between lessons I went for long walks round the Reservoir beyond my Aunt's garden. Luckily where I went was very deserted, because the whole time I was doing my vocal exercises. Over and over. And then again and again. Many of them the same exercises I do today to warm up. And gradually I built a stronger voice, and was ready to work again.

About this time, my mother returned from her wanderings, and we set up house together in a flat in Kilburn. Well it was Maida Vale if we were being posh, but usually we weren't. My faithful cat, Rebecca, who I'd brought from Lichfield, rejoiced in her new home, and quickly acquired a circle of admiring toms. (She was far too old to be spayed – an operation unnecessary for country cats, as she'd been.) They waited respectfully for her on the stone stairs that led up to the flat, when she slipped in for a bite between her prolonged bouts of lovemaking. She was hit by a bicycle, which left her with the crooked mouth of a Mona Lisa, but did not stop her ardour. We peopled North London with her kittens.

And I started working again. A strange female agent in the Kilburn High Road put me into the big Gilbert and Sullivan film, starring Robert Morley. I still looked incredibly young (for so many years I had difficulty getting served in pubs.) I found myself singing some of Sullivan's religious music, as part of a Girls' Choir. The fact that I can't sing didn't seem to matter, it was all dubbed anyway. I think we were sort of glorified extras, but it was several days' work, and it was a start. And then I got a proper film part, out at Elstree, in the Harry Alan Towers "Pickwick Papers." I think I got the interview through one of my letters. I remember going out to meet the Casting Director, and telling him he'd never seen anything as Victorian as me. He must have believed me – I played Isabella Wardle. James Donald was Jingle, and teased me unmercifully. The great Athene Seyler was Mrs. Wardle. At one of the rushes Harry Alan Towers called out, "Who's the fat girl?" At the time I was mortally wounded and upset. Looking back, I realise it was a great compliment that he'd noticed me.

And all this time I was doing "special weeks" at Reps. round London. My "party piece," which I probably played more than any other part, was Amy in "Little Women." I even managed to steal the notice from Gwen Watford, playing Jo, at Watford. I was working at Reading, catching the train every morning from Paddington, when I received a letter from the Birmingham Rep. While I was still living at Lichfield, I'd written to them frequently, with no luck or response. Now that I was based in London, they were offering me an audition for their Christmas show – Nicholas Stuart Gray's "The Princess and the Swineherd."

Reading very kindly readjusted their schedule

so that I could have a week out to go up to Birmingham for the audition. I know I was doing "The Love of Four Colonels," with them, I have a photograph of myself in a very saucy, rather Mary Queen of Scots hat. I have no idea which wife I was. From the hat, perhaps the French one?

I'd managed to get hold of a copy of the play, so I was well prepared when I read the part of the little Chinese Princess, on the stage of the oh-so-famous Birmingham Rep. for the first time. I must have done all right, as when I finished, Douglas Seale, the director, called out from the back of the steeply raked auditorium, "You'd better find yourself some digs before you go back to London..." I could hardly believe it, but it seemed I had got the part. At that time Birmingham was still at the height of its fame, and to get there was probably one of the most sought-after jobs for actors in Britain. It was not too long since Paul Schofield and Ralph Richardson had been there. And without exception all the current actors – Alan Bridges, Jack May, Richard Pascoe and Bernard Hepton, went on to make names for themselves.

Although surrounded by these luminaries, it was not a happy engagement. I loved my part, and got very good notices. (Which made one or two of the cast rather spiteful.) I loved my costume – an emerald green tunic heavily embroidered in gold, worn over emerald satin trousers. Nicholas Stuart Grey came up to see his play, a strangely fat figure of indeterminate sex. He complained bitterly that I should not be wearing trousers. However, a few years later he did employ me as a US/A.S.M. on one of his London shows – "The Marvellous History of Puss in Boots."

Sir Barry Jackson, legendary founder of the Birmingham Rep., was still alive, but he was a shadowy figure. I curtsied on the two occasions I met him, it felt appropriate, and it seemed to please him. After the dress rehearsal Douglas Seale, the director, took me aside. He said he had a message for me from Sir Barry. "Ye Gods," I thought, "What have I done?" But apparently he'd said, "Tell the child, this was how Paul Schofield made his eyes look Chinese when he played in "Lady Precious Stream" here." At that point Dougie pressed a scrap of paper into my hand. On it was a small but beautiful drawing of an eye, showing a diagonal line crossing the centre of the eyelid and carrying on at the same angle below the eye itself. Until then I'd been doing the traditional tilted black line at each corner of my eyes. This way of doing them was certainly more effective. For many years I kept and treasured the little bit of paper, but eventually it got mislaid. Along with so much else.

At that time the theatre was being run by a large and bullish lady. Everyone was in awe of her, I was terrified. Her word was law. She arranged all the contracts, as well as everything else. She had offered me £6 a week, which I'd gladly accepted, and didn't question, I was so thrilled to be going to the famous theatre. But now I was finding I simply couldn't manage. I was paying four guineas a week for B&B in a ramshackle house a long way from the theatre. Whenever I suggested moving, my aged landlady burst into tears and said she'd be destitute without my money. My mother, at home in London and still only middle-aged, refused to try to get work. She'd never been trained to do anything and having failed in her married state as an officer's wife, had no confidence at all. She did let my bedroom to students from RADA. She had Virginia Stride as a paying guest for a time. This was when John (Stride) was courting her. I gather he used to sit on the stone stairs, waiting, as the tom cats did for Rebecca. Both, presumably, having much the same idea. My mother eventually got a little part time job, sitting with the elderly mother of a lesbian lady writer. So out of my meagre earnings I sent Ma £1 a week to help out.

So there wasn't very much left to live on. And unfortunately I was still a smoker. (Bored to tears and in plaster after the riding accident in my teens, and egged on by an early boyfriend, I'd taken to sneaking Craven A from the silver box in my Grandfather's study.) But though I longed for them at Birmingham, smoking became a no-no, there was barely enough money for food, beyond my already paid for and hardly filling breakfast.

And the work was quite hard. "The Princess and the Swineherd" ran from Christmas to Easter, and we did two shows every day except Sundays. I began to feel very ill, and once or twice I fainted. (Mercifully not on stage, I always seemed all right there – thanks to Dr. Theatre.) I was advised to go and see the real company doctor. Eventually, filled with shame, I went. The doctor was affable enough, and after some routine tests, told me what I already knew – I wasn't eating enough. I tried again to move digs – more floods of tears from the landlady. I didn't see what else I could do.

But all those lovely actors in the company took matters into their own hands. Jack May – of whom I was particularly fond, went secretly to the doctor (Jack had been at Birmingham a long time, and knew him well,) to find out what was wrong with me. Alan Bridges – highly strung and intimidating, he later became a highly successful stage and television director, and was the only one who later gave me a lot of work. Anyway, Alan went to the bullish Company Manager (I wouldn't have dared approach her myself,) and asked her to give me a rise. I had discovered the other two little princesses were getting £2.50 a week more than me! But even faced with Alan, not a personality to be trifled with, Miss Boorman flatly refused to raise my salary. She argued that the other two actresses had agents who'd negotiated better deals for them (and to whom they paid commission.) Whereas I, who had no agent at the time, had accepted her offer which under no circumstances could be changed.

All this was reported to me. And then these wonderful actors took matters into their own hands. They made a rota, and each of them took me out to lunch one day a week, and paid for it – thus ensuring that I had one really good meal each day. I soon perked up and felt better. I can never thank that group of actors for their kindness, and I'm so glad each of them experienced success, each in his own way. Richard Pascoe became a much-respected stage and film actor. Bernard Hepton kept changing careers, he began as an actor, and then became a director. During this period he kept saying he would help and employ me, but nothing ever came of it. He turned back to acting, and at the end of his career found the fame he so craved. I saw him one last time, at Denville Hall, during one of my temporary incarcerations. Bernard was visiting his wife Nancy, then a long-term resident. Jack May played Collins in the television "Pride and Prejudice" when I was Mary Bennet. Even then he was anxiously scanning the racing results in the paper each morning. I believe betting finally brought about his bankruptcy and subsequent death.

Eventually I went back to London and was out of work again. At about this time I started filling in at The Gondola Coffee Bar in Wigmore Street. They advertised in "The Stage," and actually seemed to like employing actors – as waiters, even though they were apt to disappear at odd times for auditions, and leave without giving notice when they got a job. Apart from holding the record for the amount of toast I managed to burn, it was all very agreeable. And the only time I was "spotted" happened there. Someone saw my hair – back view – and wanted to photograph it for an advert. My generous employers readily agreed, and one morning I trotted off to some studio. I was paid a welcome few pounds, and months later, in some dreary waiting room, spotted my lustrous locks (back view!) in Vogue. And yes, I did tear out the page, but soon lost it.

About this time I read in The Times that the sixteenth century play "Sir Thomas More" was being accredited to Shakespeare for the first time, and published in a volume of his complete works. (Once you've been in it, you know he only wrote bits of the play. Like More's great speech, but much of it is by lesser Elizabethan hacks.) But to celebrate this event, Sir Donald Wolfit and Dorothy Sayers were going to mount a production at the Theatre Centre in St. John's Wood. Which was handily near our flat in Greville Place. (Just after we left, all the balconies fell off. They'd been loosened by bombing in the war.) I managed to get an audition with Brian Way, who was going to direct the More epic.

Before meeting him, I popped into The Times Book Club, almost next door to The Gondola, where I was still working. I riffled through the play (copies were on a huge display table,) and saw that there was the part of More's younger daughter, Cecily. As far as I could see, without buying the large volume, she only had two lines:

"See where my Father comes —
Joyful and merry."

So that was easily memorised, and Brian Way, the director, was so impressed that I actually knew the lines that he gave me the part.

A lot of fun was to follow, and I made several lasting friends in that production. Mr. Way was a great believer in improvisation. I'm not, unless you're practicing being real characters. My time rehearsing at the Theatre Centre was largely spent being a daffodil, and I wasn't very convincing – my heart wasn't in it. There was a great deal of giggling, as one of the actresses took it all with a deadly seriousness. We christened her "The Arch Tart." (Well, things went on.) And I simply couldn't see how my bulb impersonation would help with playing Cecily. Michael Beint gave a superb performance as More. Another dreadfully conscientious actress played Meg Roper, my elder sister. She pinched my arm black and blue at all the emotional bits, when our Dad was being marched off to The Tower etc. I hinted that she might try acting instead of doing it for real, but she didn't seem to know what I meant. It was that sort of production. Charles Lewson, still a schoolboy at Westminster, played a minor part but joined in all the corpsing (laughing on stage) with gusto.

We did three performances in period costumes, and three in modern dress. The Elizabethan cozzies came from Sir Donald Wolfit's theatre collection, and were decidedly musty. For the up-to-date ones I wore the dress I'd made while I was at the Birmingham Rep. (with a lot of help from the Wardrobe mistress.) Sir Donald supervised while we tried on his costumes, while Dorothy Sayers hovered and looked on, occasionally making some penetrating criticism. I didn't find Sir Donald as frightening as I expected... (I'd made the pilgrimage to Camden Town to marvel at his "Lear,") but his voice boomed round the smallish space where we were to play. Much to my relief he agreed that it was all right for me to wear my (at that time longish) hair loose for the performances, since Cecily was unmarried. The Theatre Centre was near enough to our flat for members of the cast to come back for coffee, after our improvisation sessions. It was very interesting to have played in "Sir Thomas More," even if not very much of it was by Shakespeare, and altogether it was a very jolly experience.

Christmas came round again, and Nicholas Stuart Gray remembered me from Birmingham, and offered me a job as Understudy and A.S.M. on his West End production of "Puss in Boots." This was to be at The Fortune Theatre, with a wonderful cast headed by Joy Parker, Paul Schofield's wife. (Alas, I never saw him, and very little of her. They were such a private couple.) And it wasn't a very happy engagement for me. The young Stage Manager, my immediate superior, seemed intent on making my life a misery. I expect I was very trying, my heart had never been in stage management, all I wanted to do was act. Before one performance I played "God Save The Queen" twice on the panatrope, and the audience dutifully rose to its feet twice, too. (Those were the days!) Nicholas Stuart Gray just laughed when he heard, but the young man, rightly, was furious with me. I understudied the two ladies in waiting to the Princess (Joy Parker's part.) After understudy rehearsals this Stage Manager always reported that I didn't know my lines. In fact I was D.L.P. (dead letter perfect.) It was just that these two characters talked exclusively to each other and no one else. I was the only person at the rehearsals, and it was one long double act of me talking to myself and answering back... I had no desire to play either of the parts, and mercifully didn't have to "go on." I regret to say I became so miserable I took my woes to the Stage Director, Bernard Gillman. He was very sweet and understanding, and listened sympathetically to my grievances. Some real, some imagined. Luckily "Puss in Boots" was only on for a short Christmas run.

Later on, when he was manager of The Arts Theatre, Bernard Gillman cast me as one of the schoolgirls in the first London production of "The Children's Hour." This was the controversial play about lesbians by Lillian Hellman. The Lord Chamberlain still held sway over the London Theatre, and it was only possible to put it on because the Arts was a club. Margo Van der Burgh and Rosalie Crutchley played the leads. The part of the Grandmother of the evil little girl, Mary, who makes all the trouble, was taken by Bessie Love. She had been a star of silent films, and was an ardent Christian Scientist. She used to come into our dressing room, and lecture us (as we were only playing small parts we had long waits.) Bessie assured us we need never be out of work – we could join amateur groups and help others etc. I'm afraid Pekoe Ainley and I rather pulled faces behind her back at this advice. Pekoe and I became friends during the production, she always seemed in awe and rather overpowered by her famous rampaging actor father, Richard. Frances Guthrie was also in our dressing room. She took Bessie's lectures completely seriously. Being so tiny, Frances did very well playing real child parts, including Wendy in "Peter Pan." (Early on I broke my heart wanting to play Wendy. I always had too much bosom.)

Much against my will, I continued acting teenagers until I was well into my thirties. But a job was a job, and the rent had to be paid. When I was long past the age for playing it, an agent sent me for an audition for the schoolgirl in "Wait Until Dark." I didn't know this had been a famous Audrey Hepburn film, and the job was hardly alluring – a special week in Rotherham. I met the director, Richard Carey, and we seemed to share the same sense of humour. I didn't know until later, but apparently he told the people putting on this epic, that unless the girl who'd made him laugh at the audition played the schoolgirl he wouldn't do the production.

So I got the part, and struggled into my mother's gymslip one last time. We all went up to Rotherham, and I got digs in a Victorian pub. Downstairs by the bar was bright and cheerful enough. But on the deserted upper floor, where my room was, it was extremely dark and smelt of mould and decay. A single bare bulb swung eerily in the draughts. But the theatre was quite newly built and supposed to be modern. The architect had forgotten to put in any dressing rooms – so they'd been added as an afterthought, and were certainly no better than those to be found in any nineteenth century theatre. Architects never seem to consider the vast amounts of time actors have to spend there, and no one seems even to consider making them comfortable.

Hardly surprisingly "Wait Until Dark" didn't do much business in Rotherham. I supposed everyone had seen the film... So lots of tickets were given away. The landlord of the pub where I was staying got some. He was far too busy serving and making merry with the locals, so he gave the tickets to the tarts who congregated in the bar every night. I was already on nodding terms with them, so after the show I eagerly sought their opinion.

It came, swift and cutting, from their vermillion-haired spokeswoman: "Ee, lass, you're never going t'make it in showbiz...Why don't you join us?" Probably the best offer I've ever had, but I did refuse it.

My bosom also came to the fore, so to speak, when another agent sent me to audition for yet another television "Alice." The aforementioned of course ruled me out from the main part, but along with all the other aspiring young actresses (they were all from various stage schools like Sylvia Young) I was hived off as an animal... Once again I was to be in fur for Christmas. I told my friends they'd be able to spot me, as among all the nymphets, I'd be "the only rabbit with a bosom."

The fur was hot, as of course the Christmas "Alice" was shot in midsummer. My part was small, and I can recall only one incident of any interest.

The Duchess was played with consummate art (and vulgarity) by the inimitable Peter Bull. (A performance I never saw equalled until many years later, when Simon Russell Beale stole the show and danced the part for The Royal Ballet.) I was having lunch on location, and the whole table was listening to one of Peter's stories, when his false nose came off and fell into his soup! I have no doubt this became another of the tales he recounted so brilliantly.

So when Christmas time really came, despite appearing in "The Radio Times" in very small print, us rabbits were listed as "Other parts played by…" I was once more looking for work. Completely desperate, and knowing I can't sing, I even went to audition for the pantomime "Little Red Riding Hood" at the old Dinely Studios, near Baker Street.

While waiting my turn for the rejection to my, "I'm so sorry. No, I don't sing…" I overheard two other actresses talking. My ears flapped. I gathered they'd just been to an audition for a Christmas play at Toynbee Hall. A children's play – that was more in my line than panto. I leaned forward, and caught that the director was someone called Stephen Joseph. By then I'd heard enough. I didn't wait for my summary dismissal by the pantomime people. I went straight home and rang Toynbee Hall, which I knew was somewhere in the East End. Whoever answered the phone said yes, she supposed Mr. Joseph would be coming in the next morning. I thanked her, and rang off.

I set off very early the following day. I'd found

out where Toynbee Hall was, and went to Aldgate East and walked from there. A cleaner obligingly let me in. Soon after ten o'clock Stephen Joseph appeared. I recognised him at once, there was such a striking resemblance to his mother, Hermione Gingold. Trying not to sound sheepish, I explained that I'd heard about the play (which, it turned out, was called "Smugglers Beware") and wanted to audition. With the utmost courtesy Stephen took me into the office and allowed me to read for the leading girl, Henrietta. And yes, I got the part. It seemed Stephen thought Henrietta, as written, rather wet, and was looking for someone feisty to give it character. My gate crashing the audition showed the sort of spunk Stephen wanted. Contracts were exchanged, and rehearsals started the following Monday.

It was a lovely cast, and everyone was very friendly. My little brother was played by Fella Edmunds, a boy film star of the time. Stephen was a splendid director, and kept everyone in good spirits. He was such a wonderful man − he'd introduced theatre-in-the-round into this country, and fought to establish it against so many obstacles and difficulties. He founded the famous theatre at Scarborough, now the home and jumping-off ground of Alan Ayckbourn. For many years Stephen was aided and helped by the dramatist David Campton, who became my life-long friend.

I gathered that "Smugglers Beware" was being financed by an Australian sheep farmer. He'd arranged to put it on in London so that his girlfriend, a budding actress and model, could play Henrietta. Luckily for me, she'd landed some other, more lucrative, job.

So we were all quite unprepared for the blow which fell on the third day of rehearsals. Grim-faced, Stephen called all the cast together as we arrived at 10.30. It seemed the girlfriend had decided that she did want to play Henrietta after all. "Not, of course, that she's going to – " announced Stephen. "I chose Pamela to play Henrietta, and she's under contract to do so." Stephen continued, "Sadly, I must suspend rehearsals while this matter is cleared up. Go home and study your parts. I shall expect everyone to be D.L.P. when we resume, and I'll call you when we can restart. Thank you, everyone, for your good work so far." Everyone grabbed for their coats. I was putting mine on when Stephen took my arm. "Not you – " he said. "You and me are going to have a little private strike."

Stephen led me to the nearby ABC and ordered coffees. "We're going to sit here, in working hours, for as long as it takes the management to come to their senses. No director, no rehearsals, the play doesn't go on. Of course he's offered to pay you in full – but I'm not buying that. You've signed a contract to play Henrietta, and you will play her. I have to teach this man that he can't just buy people off."

So for three days Stephen and I sat together in the ABC, and I listened to his fascinating conversation. "You must always praise actors, they have so little self-confidence. Especially praise the bad ones – then even they will improve" and "Never wear completely flat shoes on stage. You'll walk like a duck..."

After three days the manager caved in, rehearsals started again and I was once more enjoying playing Henrietta. Stephen remained a friend for the rest of his tragically short life. (He died of cancer of the liver at the early age of forty five.) Knowing he was dying, he asked all his friends, in twos and threes, to stay at his house in Scarborough for a few days. David Campton and I, now almost an item, went for a sad yet wonderfully inspiring weekend. It happened that Stephen and I had a call to the bathroom at the same time in the middle of the night. We met in a dark corridor, and the final "goodbyes" were said. "But please – " he implored me, "Don't marry David. It won't work. Just be good friends." I assured him that that was how it was going to be, and would remain.

I have one other marvellous memory of Stephen. I was always going to go up to Scarborough for the season, but I had to wait until there were the right parts. (I was always difficult to cast in repertory. Often I looked far too young. Hence the great number of "special weeks" I did – usually playing teenagers.) Then one year it happened, there were parts I could play at Stephen's in-the-round theatre. Stephen asked me, well in advance, for his summer season, and of course I accepted. Then, much nearer the date when rehearsals in Scarborough were due to commence, I was offered the part of Mary Bennet in the BBC-TV serial production of "Pride and Prejudice." And the dates clashed with the season at Scarborough. With trepidation I rang Stephen and told him. "Don't be silly – " he said warmly. "Pride and Prejudice" happens once in a person's life. Of course, take it. You can come to us anytime." But there wasn't another time. He died later that year. Thank you, Stephen, for so much.

CHAPTER EIGHT

1959

So I did "Pride and Prejudice" on telly. I got it because I'd already done another television serial – "Villette" for the director, Barbara Burnham.

That production was almost the first thing I did on television. And I got into that through the kindness of David Willmot. I'd known him when he was an A.S.M. at Windsor. He moved on to become a Floor Manager at the BBC. One morning he met Barbara Burnham in a corridor. "Where can I find an actress who looks young enough to be a schoolgirl and speaks some French?" Apparently she was almost distraught. She added, "I can't use a real child – ". And David suggested me, and I successfully auditioned and got the part. The lead, Lucy Snow, was played by the wonderful Jill Bennett. There was a classroom scene where I had to heckle her in French. It wasn't very difficult. But then Jill had to punish me, twisting my neck and pushing me into a cupboard. I remember the enormous concern Jill showed – she was afraid she'd hurt me. At rehearsals I kept saying, "No. Harder – harder. Do it for real –". In those days all television was done live – nothing was recorded. We did the serials on Sunday night, and went back and did it all over again for the Thursday repeat. As there could be no pauses between scenes, often you ran from set to set, changing your costume as you went. In an episode of "Villette" I remember Jill arriving, breathless, for a scene, and instantly realising that the chair that should have been set for her at the table wasn't there. Without a second's hesitation she bent her knees in a pretend sitting position, and held the position for the entire scene. I'm sure no one who was watching at home realised anything was wrong.

But then, before I even started rehearsing for "Pride and Prejudice," the BBC did the meanest of mean things to me. At that time I was also playing small parts in Tennent's very prestigious television productions. These were made out at Elstree under the general directorship of Cecil Clarke. I came to be in these because Peter Potter's partner saw me in a BBC-TV play about the Penge Murders. Reluctantly Peter agreed to see me, and at the interview remarked that his partner thought I was the greatest thing on television since sliced bread! Despite this sarcasm, he employed me in some nice little parts. I played The Scullery Maid in "The Wild Bird," with Leslie Caron in the lead. (I'd noted with interest that she wrote in her autobiography… "A girl never outgrows her mother's opinion of her." I lived to know the truth of this statement.) Hugh Griffiths had been engaged to play her father, and I watched, fascinated, as Miss Caron did battle with him in this Anouilh piece. I'd thought of Hugh Griffiths as an actor of genius, and was thrilled to have the chance of watching him rehearse. But he had a reputation for hitting the bottle and being unsure of his lines. Within days Miss Caron got him dismissed, using the excuse that she was acting in English, which was only a second language for her, and she couldn't risk an actor who gave her duff cues. So Hugh was replaced by Maurice Denham, peerless on radio, otherwise a safe, steady good actor. But watching Hugh, as I'd been privileged to do, was as they said of Kean's acting, "illuminated by flashes of lightning."

When I'd already got the contract from the BBC for the five episodes of "Pride and Prejudice" I was to be in, Cecil Clarke offered me the part of The Maidservant opposite Mary Morris (a heroine of mine) in John Masefield's "The Witch." It was to be a hugely prestigious Tennent's television production, and was one of the few big chances to come my way. But the dates almost collided with "Pride and Prejudice." Unfortunately I hadn't got an agent to negotiate this tricky situation for me, so I rang Cecil Clarke myself. He could not have been more accommodating, it seemed they really wanted me for the part. He and the BBC agreed (admittedly the Beeb somewhat reluctantly,) that I was to rehearse "Pride and Prejudice" in the mornings, and go to "The Witch" in the afternoons. There were to be six episodes of the Jane Austen, but I wasn't in number five. And had not been contracted to do it. And this was the production week of "The Witch," so I could be with Tennent's full time. It all fitted in perfectly, and I still have the letter of agreement from Cecil

Clarke. And then the BBC dropped its bombshell. They suddenly announced that I was to be in episode five after all. In fact, they wrote in an extra two lines for me. I learnt afterwards that the Beeb didn't want me popping up on the other channel when I was appearing in their precious classic serial. But it was a mean trick, and I know who was responsible. She's still around in the theatre world. I believe she calls herself an agent.

So I began "Pride and Prejudice" with a grudge against the BBC. I've often thought that if only I'd had a good agent at the time, they would have upheld the original contract and seen to it that I did both jobs. Maybe... But the cast of "Pride and Prejudice" were so wonderful I was soon immersed in playing Mary. Our parents, Mr. and Mrs. Bennet, were played by the splendiferous Marion Spencer and Hugh Sinclair. Hugh travelled up from Lewes every day, with much grumbling about the trains. He explained that actors of his generation, including William Squire who was also in the serial, moved their families away from London for the sake of their children. In their heyday their careers had consisted solely of long runs of West End plays, which meant they only had to travel up to London for the evening performances. They simply hadn't thought of television and having to spend all day in London studios. Before the weekly recording of each episode, we all used to have supper together in the canteen at the old Lime Grove studios. We would pull several tables together, with Hugh and Marion at the head, and all us Bennet girls, their daughters, sitting round. Elizabeth was played by lovely red-haired Jane Downs, and the highly talented Vivien Merchant was Lydia.

Ours was the second time the BBC had televised "Pride and Prejudice." (Prunella Scales played Lydia in the first one.) But it was said ours was the one that would be remembered, as we had the definitive Darcy in the superb actor Alan Badel. Alan had a natural haughty demeanour that just was Darcy, he didn't need to act. (Nor did he need to dive, half-naked, into a lake, to be convincing.) To begin with I found him rather frightening, but soon discovered he was the kindest of men. He played many parts in the West End – "Kean" was probably one of his greatest performances. Alan ran his own theatrical company. Some weeks after we finished the serial, I wrote to him with my usual request – to be considered for work. His reply was a letter to be treasured, he said he and his wife had been watching reruns of "Pride and Prejudice" (so it was recorded!) and after watching my performance as Mary, if the right part came along, it would be mine without auditioning. Sadly no such part turned up, and before too many years had passed, Alan was dead.

I'd got into the classic serials originally by writing (and writing) to Chloe Gibson. Chloe gave me one of those walk-ons, with no lines, that's almost a part. I was thrilled to be The Innkeeper's daughter in the first episode of "Kenilworth." Especially as Mine Host himself was played by Arthur Brough, (I remembered, though didn't mention it to him, being taken to one of Arthur's Tea Matinées at the Rep. in Folkestone, when I was at school there. A rare treat.) Arthur found fame very late in life when he starred on television in "Are you Being Served?"

Some of this episode was filmed in the stable yard at Oswestry. I'd visited the house several times on Sunday afternoon outings. Suddenly the yard was as I'd always imagined it, bustling with horses and carriages and people in period costume. I dodged in and out with a tray of drinks. It was all so real. I felt I was living, breathing, existing, in the past. It isn't often you feel this level of reality in acting. Just before the first take Arthur said to me, "Don't whatever you do, forget your lines!"

Other BBC-TV classic serials followed. I was in "The Eustace Diamonds," adapted from Trollope's great novel. The lead, Lord Fawn, was played by Robert Edison, a good actor. He always seemed rather aloof and distant, but he gave a brilliant performance in this epic. Angela Crowe, Carol Marsh and I played the Fawn sisters. I read the book, and discovered that Trollope described them as "the ugliest girls in the south of England." The others weren't pleased when I told them. Our Mother was played by Jean Cadell. She became quite motherly towards us, and was always complaining about our costumes. As upper-class "gals" she thought we should be wearing smarter dresses. I don't know if she actually complained to Wardrobe, but when we got to Episode Four, we were suddenly promoted to much grander cozzies.

Jean Cadell voiced her approval. "At last my daughters are decently turned out!" she exclaimed.

For most of the classic serials the BBC used rehearsal rooms at Wormwood Scrubs. Near the prison was a great grassed-over open space, and the King's Troupe used it regularly to exercise their horses. As I travelled there and back on various buses, I used to keep a sharp lookout for the wonderful cavalcade, and was often rewarded by the sight of all the mounted troops and their beautiful chargers, saddles, bridles and every piece of equipment gleaming in the morning sun. (Well, sometimes, you know the English weather.) Once, going home on the bus when I was doing "Pride and Prejudice," I travelled with the great actress from a bygone age, Phyllis Neilson-Terry, who was, suitably, playing Lady Catherine de Burgh. I was delighted to hear her reply, when confronted by the conductor. She boomed, in her deep contralto voice that carried to the back of the gallery, "Paddington, if you please, wherever that may be..." I doubt if the astonished conductor even managed to give her a ticket.

At that time all the BBC classic serials were directed by either Chloe Gibson or Barbara Burnham. They both seemed enormously old to me, I suppose they were in their late fifties. Both smoked (Barbara had been known to set her trouser turn-ups alight,) had grey hair and heavily painted nails. Since neither of them ever had time to let it set properly, their red varnish was always wrinkled. But quite apart from all the lovely parts she gave me, I have a great reason to be grateful to Barbara. At that time I had several quite large moles on my face. One day, towards the end of "Pride and Prejudice," she took me on one side for a confidential chat. After telling me how pleased she was with my work as Mary Bennet, she mentioned my moles. She said, "I've been able to shoot you all right. But I must warn you, television is about to change. We shall be using much stronger cameras, the close-up will be paramount. Everything will be shot in close-up. You must get those moles on your face removed now, and you'll do very well in the future."

At the time I had a most agreeable GP, and he readily agreed to send me to St. Mary's to have them removed on the NHS. Although it involved a full anaesthetic it was quite a small operation. I had a very good surgeon who took an enormous amount of care of my face, insisting on coming up to the ward (I stayed in overnight) to take the stitches out himself. So everything seemed to be very satisfactory.

Except that a few days later I noticed a small swelling on my forehead, up by my hairline. I'd always had a tiny, hardly noticeable scar there – the relic of half a brick my brother had thrown at me, for not being able to sing in tune! Unfortunately this swelling, which had a dark centre, was now very enlarged. So I went back to my nice doctor who arranged for me to see the same surgeon. After it had been removed (another night in hospital) the slightly amazed surgeon said that even small operations, like the mole removal, can cause upheavals. There'd been a speck of coal dust lurking in my forehead ever since Peter had heaved the brick — the operation had brought it to the surface, but it was now safely removed.

But I had got penicillin poisoning. I'd had on a warning red bracelet, but it must have been obscured by the blanket when the drug was generally administered to all who'd had ops. that morning. I was starting to turn brown by the time I got home. Soon it spread all over. I looked like Guy the Gorilla. Alas — I'd been overdosed with the-then-new wonder drug after the riding accident. On this occasion Marje rushed me back to the hospital in a taxi; and my condition was soon brought under control by several large doses of antihistamines. Gradually my skin returned to its normal colouring, and all was well.

CHAPTER NINE

Life after the accident

2006

My dreary hours of constrained living in only two rooms continued: wake up; long for cup of tea, but of course unable to make it up to the kitchen. Wonder if any carers will turn up today? And when? Drag myself out of bed for a strip wash – best I can do. Quite a lot of pain, so have to lie on bed for a bit before I struggle into some clothes. Have a nice bracing drink of cold water – at least that bottle's within reach. Lie on the bed and do my exercises. Was that the buzzer? No, but maybe someone will come in an hour, or two. Clean the pins, disinfect everywhere, use the machine, tighten the screws. Oh, the pain.

Perhaps John will come today. Or Michael or Pauline. Thank God for visitors. There's the buzzer – I have a Carer! Now I'll get that cup of tea and something to eat. What can I ask her to buy in the hour's shopping that I'm allowed each week? Eggs – they're always a good bet. No wonder I don't put on weight. They weigh me every time I go to the hospital. When's my next visit? At least I'll smell fresh air as they carry me to the ambulance and get a glimpse of the outside world through the tiny windows. Oh let me write something – anything, and dear John will type it. One day I'll get better. One day I'll walk again.

When I was in bed last night, as always, listening to the radio, they played an excerpt from "Bohème." The usual bit from Act I, "your tiny hand is frozen," etc. I didn't know who the Mimi was – not Mirella Freni – she was the best of all, tiny, fragile, that soaring voice, she just was Mimi, she'd made the part her own. And Domingo, of course, it's always Domingo. Such a lovely man, and I drifted off, remembering my very beginnings of working at The Opera House.

And it all began because I went down to Southampton to do a telly. It was either a Schools or a University production, anyway highly educational. Also in it was an actress called Jane Evers. We were, respectively, the wives to Ham and Shem (I suppose Japhet also had a wife but I can't remember who she was.) The voice of God was played by a wonderful old actor who kept saying how lovely we were when we drowned, and on the monitor you only saw our little hands bobbing above the water. (I thought everyone in the Ark was saved, but maybe we were being other people by then.) But as we were staying away from home for the few days it took to make this epic, Jane and I had plenty of time to talk. Firstly, we discovered that we lived within five minutes of each other in London.

And I found out that Jane worked as an "extra," or actress, as they were called even back then, at the Royal Opera House, Covent Garden.

Once back in London and living so near to each other, our friendship grew. We took to meeting in our local pub and treating each other to ciders, and discussing our careers (such as they were.) More often than not, Jane would be clutching a little brown envelope containing, in cash, her week's wages from the Opera House. Fairly soon, we knew each other well enough to admit we really preferred coffee to cider and we took to meeting in Jane's flat nearby. And I would watch enviously as she filled in her various engagements at the Opera House in an enormous diary. And, "Can't I do that?" became, from me, an almost continual refrain.

So Jane told me to write to Stella Chitty, doyenne Stage Manager of the Royal Opera House, who did the casting of the actors for the various productions. So I wrote to Stella, religiously, every three months – she always replied, and her reply was always the same – I was too small and she already had all her "old" (and that included Jane who was a favourite of hers) actors to look after.

And then, one November day in 1983, I received a different typed letter. It wondered if I would care to audition for Mr. John Copley's new production of "La Bohème?" Would I??!! I hastily scanned the pages of the Pan Book of Opera. It seemed there were Milkmaids. I was too ignorant to know these were sung by members of the chorus. As I'd been so repeatedly told I was too small, I could only think the Rodolfo was five foot and they wanted munchkins. (In fact, it was Domingo.) But on the day of the audition, I turned up suitably dressed. There were many actors and actresses waiting in the dress circle and I spotted one or two old friends, including David Rowley – we'd been at the Mermaid together. Very soon a rumour came back from the beautiful Crush Bar (now demoted to be the mundane Crush Room) where the audition was being held. It said that they were only looking for one girl and she had to be 5'10", dark, and speaking fluent Italian. As a blonde, struggling to reach 5'2", my heart and hopes sank. But my Guardian Angel must have been looking after me. I went in with two quite well-known actresses, Amanda, daughter of Stephen Murray, and Carol Marsh, who'd been discovered for the film "Alice" and made "Brighton Rock." Stella Chitty introduced John – small, bespectacled, bubbling over with enthusiasm – who told us a few things about his upcoming production. Then he asked us to move about (we'd been sitting) so that he could have a look at us. And that was where my luck held. The two name actresses, for reason known only to themselves (I presumed they didn't want the job) remained firmly seated. I got up and waltzed round and round John, saying things like "Lots of blondes in Paris" (at least I knew that was the setting of Bohème) and "Berlitz Lesson 12 in Italian." (Also true, that was as far as I got.) But it made John laugh. He said "Stop it Pamela – you're making me dizzy." My audition was over.

A week or two later, I received a telephone called from the formidable Stella Chitty. "Miss Binns," she said coldly, "I have good news for you." "You mean I'm coming?" I nearly fell off the end of the phone. "We had to change the whole casting for you." Her voice was even more frigid. "What am I playing?" There was a great rustling of papers. "Fluffy Lady No.2. Fluffy Lady No.1 will be Pauline Stroud." I was working this out. Pauline Stroud, who made "Lady Godiva Rides Again." And Stella was telling me that I'd be receiving details about coming for a costume fitting in due course. And that was it. I was going to be an actress at the Royal Opera House in Mr. John Copley's new production of "La Bohème."

I received my call to come for a costume fitting at 45 Floral Street (just opposite the stage door) early in December. I went in my little sky blue Mini, suitably called Eyr. I drove everywhere about London in those heady days. It was the time of the "three-day week" – you only had precious electricity three days a week. I found a meter and couldn't remember if it was an off-day, or if I had to put money in. In the end, I just left it (and it was OK) and made my way to Floral Street. The door was open and I went along a dark passage. A nice woman in a bright pinafore took me into a small room crammed with costumes. In those days cozzies, accounts, everything, was run from small offices at No. 45. I stripped off and the fitter said, "You're very small," approvingly. After she'd tied a vast hooped petticoat round my waist (at least I was used to doing period work) she produced 'The Dress'. "I think you'll be able to wear this." She was smiling now. "It's very special. We believe it was in the Melba production of "Bohème" at the turn of the century. Probably worn by one of the chorus. They don't weave cotton thinly like that anymore – you feel it –" And indeed, the cotton, sprigged with white flowers, was almost gauze-like. The dress was completed with a white lace collar and cuffs. I was given an apron and cap to transform me into the Grisette, as the fluffy ladies had now become. And then everything, to my mind, was ruined by the addition of a hideous brown velvet coat. I was given a thick shawl as my 'disguise' for Act III, whatever that was going to be...

And I rejoiced, and could hardly believe my eyes, when that same dress came back for the 39th revival for me to wear, as the Elegant Lady, in December 2013. My dress, stiffened and completely relined, now with a lace inset down the front and, of course, let out, had been in so many other opera productions, rented out, and travelled the world. She'd just come back from some production in Spain. Oh, if only 'my' dress could talk! But at least, at last, we were reunited. Oh the joy of getting into her again. So much had happened in the intervening years.

I got my first call in early January 1974. In those days all the rehearsals were held in the London Opera Centre, a converted cinema in the East End, way out beyond Aldgate – a long and tedious journey for those having to use public transport. I was so lucky being able to go in my Mini. I'd made a trial run the previous Sunday and, as there was no traffic to speak of, had found my way without difficulty. But Monday morning in the rush hour was quite different. I went wrong at the Mansion House. Luckily, a smiling policeman held everyone else up while I righted the Mini. I pulled up outside the Opera Centre and, with some trepidation, I entered the building. Eventually I was directed down to the large studio in the basement. It was crowded with people. Later I learnt they were mainly the chorus. Someone, an ASM, found me, ticked me off on the list and introduced me to my partner, John Wilding. A big burly man, not much of an actor, but so kind. Awhile later, when we were rehearsing something else, somewhere else, I had 'flu, and in the break, John carried me, bodily, to a nearby café, plonked me on a chair and produced a cup of steaming hot chocolate. Such a generous man, and an embryo playwright. We had a month's rehearsal for that first production, and with Pauline and her partner, Rodney, we killed many hours in the canteen at the Opera Centre. We gave spirited readings from bits of John's plays and he got us playing lots of pencil and paper games. Once I pretended to read their palms, but Roddy got quite upset, so I never did it again. I'd been introduced to Pauline, earlier, little realising we were to be linked together for the next forty years.

Stella clapped her hands for silence, and gradually the hubbub subsided. John began explaining about Act II, the Café Momus, which everybody was in. He began showing people where their opening positions would be – either in the café itself, or outside in the street (that's where all the sellers were, of course.) Pauline and I were to be seated at one of the tables. At last, everyone was settled and the exciting opening chords were played on the piano. And one of the very first moves John gave was to me. I was to take Pauline's hand and run out of the café. Everything had happened so quickly, I had no idea of the cue. I was used to being in straight plays with perhaps three or four people on the stage. Now, surrounded by nearly a hundred, and all the street sellers bawling their wares, I was completely lost in the cacophony of sounds. John clapped his hands and said, "Back." And we did the same bit all over again, and I still hadn't the faintest idea when to move. I had no idea that early opera rehearsals are like this. You do a few bars, and then go back over it. Again. And again. And I remained frozen to my chair. (And a memory flicked somewhere at the back of my brain, of being a Powder Puff in a dancing display when I was very small and nearly wetting myself with anxiety as I couldn't recognise my music cue. In the event, I think someone pushed me. I believe my poor Father, just back from serving in India, was forced into watching this shameful display. Was any of this grounds for the eventual divorce?)

Meanwhile, John, seemingly in disgust, had turned his attention to other matters. Someone lesser from the stage management led Pauline and me to the Repetiteur, seated at the piano in the corner. He was reading "The Hobbit." What seems to be the trouble?" he enquired mildly. I explained that I was having difficulty picking up the cue to move. He played it over a few times, and said, "There!" None the wiser, and sure that my career in opera was about to end before it had begun, I made my way back to the table. Pauline, looking like the Beauty Queen she'd once been, gave him a Princess-Diana-sideways-under-the-lashes look and followed me. I'd hardly sat down before the dark-haired chorus lady sitting next to me whispered, "Don't worry, I'll touch your foot. Just get up and go when you feel it." Wonderful Anne Guthrie gave me that cue for years afterwards, though I learned it quite quickly enough once I got used to being in opera. As well as being a lovely person and singer, all through the years she was in the chorus she was always helping and teaching me things. I remember when we were rehearsing "Maria Stuarda" her saying, "And this one's an aria, Pam, and this is a cavatina..."

The days of rehearsing just with the chorus passed very quickly. Then, one exciting morning, I pulled the Mini up next to a grand coffee-coloured Rolls. A tall, bronzed man with tightly curly hair was being helped out by a chauffeur. I didn't recognise Domingo but followed him in. We came to the huge studio crammed with people all talking at the tops of their voices. But a hush came over them on Domingo's entrance. I tucked myself away in a corner. John Copley rushed forward and introduced the great tenor. Everyone clapped.

At that time, I hadn't been told that we – the actors – must treat the principals like Royalty i.e. we must never address them unless they spoke to us first. Ignorant of this ruling, one morning I trotted up to Domingo – he seemed so nice – and asked him how he was? He cleared his throat before answering: "I hava de throat. And at-a-de weekend I hava to sing in Hambourg." I pointed to the gold medallion of St. Cecilia he wore round his neck. "Surely she will look after you?" I suggested. The great tenor shrugged. "I 'ope so. Sincerely, I 'ope so –" After the weekend I asked him how his recital had gone? Once again, with the utmost courtesy, he assured me all had been well with his voice. No wonder this man is loved by everyone in the opera world, indeed loved all over the world.

One by one the other principals arrived. John introduced us to the famous baritone, Peter Glossop, who was singing Marcello. It was with him we were to do our bit of acting. He would pick us up, take us downstage and attempt to kiss Pauline. And I, more of a Puritan, would pull her away. Peter Glossop shook his great lion's mane of auburn hair and growled, "They won't be able to do it!" "Of course they will," contradicted John. "They're both proper actresses. I chose them myself." But Glossop shrugged his shoulders and walked away. Of course I learnt the words and the music, and we subsequently did it over the next two decades with every famous baritone who sang at the Garden.

Katia Ricciarelli was the next arrival. Though her voice was already beautiful, she was comparatively inexperienced. Her claim to the rôle of Mimi was her triumph in a number of singing competitions in Italy. She came in shyly, wearing a most unbecoming black velvet jockey cap, far from the poised and beautiful young woman she became a few years later. Peter Glossop said loudly, "Cor, she has got an arse." Really guaranteed to make the pool girl feel at home. The cast was completed by Thomas Allen in the smaller rôle of Schaunard.

We came to the first day actually on the stage at Covent Garden. We were going to do Act II, the Café Momus scene. I made my way through the market to the Opera House. I asked the stage door keeper the way to the canteen. He pointed. I descended cavernous passageways into the bowels of the earth. I followed a few desultory notices saying 'Restaurant.' I finally sat at a table with a cup of coffee. I was joined by the only other new actor, Raymond. We clutched each other and giggled. First day at school again. I said, "Have you found the loo?" He hadn't. He said, "Have you signed in?" Of course I hadn't. With difficulty I wound my way back to the stage door.

A bell rang, and what seemed like 100 people streamed towards the stage. Someone said, "Wait for the lift." It's tiny and takes ages. I managed to change into my ballet shoes in the scrum being propelled upwards. I asked Pauline where we left our bags. She said, "Throw them into the wings." I ran across the stage – it seemed smaller than I expected – and took my place at a table in the Café Momus. There's Ann – my lovely soprano.

Julia Trevelyan Oman's set is perfect — crumbling Paris in the 1840's — it resembles a Foujita painting. As well as the upstairs billiard room in the café, the streets outside are on several different levels. No detail has been omitted. There are stuffed rabbits and plucked chickens on the poultry stall. Copies of period jewellery in the adjoining shops in the crowded alley at the back of the set, and the chestnut man's brazier was belching out smoke only too realistically. In his tiny kitchen, Mark Allington, who played the Cook so brilliantly, was preparing the meal. Mark never missed a performance in all the years we did "Bohème". John Wilding and I made the first street level. It was too congested to move so we kissed at the bottom of the stairs, to the accompaniment of rude remarks from the chorus. Musetta came on without her wig but with the Peke. Alcindoro entered without make-up, looking all of twenty-eight. No one was singing out. The curtain fell. But there was still twenty-three minutes of precious Musicians' Union time so we went back to the beginning of the act yet again.

At last the rehearsal was over. Having changed, I went to have a drink at the bar with Pauline and Mary Morse-Boycott, who plays the little old lady behind the cash desk in the Café Momus. (The part I took over for the very last revival.) A glass of wine went straight to my head. John Copley floated by, "John —" I said, desperately, "The coat —." "Oh, Mimi's wasn't it awful —? That's been killed." "No, mine, John, it's dreadful. I look

like Whistler's Mother — couldn't we get rid of it?"
Enigmatic look, followed by peals of laughter.
"Darling, we'll have to ask Julia." The following day
I heard that the brilliant designer had agreed for me
to wear my shawl instead of the hated coat. Thrown
over my shoulders and secured with a nappy pin, I
wore it like that for all my years of playing the
Grisette.

Much later Pauline and I walked through the
Market and picked up discarded vegetables on our
way home. We both got some very phallic carrots,
she got a lemon and I found a turnip. We have each
been given an amphitheatre ticket for the public
dress rehearsal. A few days later the Stage
Manager, Stella Chitty, caught me at my vegetable
scrounging. "Don't we pay you enough, Miss
Binns?" she asked icily.

And then, suddenly it was the public dress-
rehearsal. I arrived very early, and was somewhat
alarmed to find the Friends' queue already
stretching away down Bow Street. I went to the
canteen for a coffee. Back to the dressing-room —
people streaming everywhere. There is a security
guard in the corridor saying, "I've instructions only to
let friends of Mr. Domingo..." Sounds of real
singing. Katia warming up, I think. It sent shivers
down my spine. Also all the noise from the crowd
outside. Our dressing-room is just below street
level and we could see all the feet passing the
window. Pantechnicons in Floral Street were
moving out Saturday night's scenery, and rails of
costumes were being wheeled forward and back

across the road.

Gradually we all got dressed and made-up. The singing sounded lovely over the tannoy. Act I went much more quickly than we'd expected – twenty minutes, and our call came. I went up to the prompt side with Mary M-B., I still can't find my way by myself. Waited as instructed, with several chorus ladies, back by the door, while the stage hands moved the huge twenty-foot flats perilously close by us. The Waiters and our boyfriends were carrying the tables and chairs on to the stage.

At last we were called to our places. There was only just time to arrange my dress. The familiar chords from the brass and the great curtains parted. I ran and took Pauline's hand, we went out of the café into the street dutifully shivering and pulling our shawls round us, though no one can see.

We fought our way through the massing bodies. No time to do any business now. The singing sounded very loud here on the stage. Looked out for Peter Glossop. There he was straight ahead. We listened for "lo pur mi sento in vena di gridar." I was there, on his left arm. I kept my eyes fixed on his. His massive lion's mane of curls descended on Pauline as he kissed her. I dragged her away and she cannoned into dear Thomas Allen who had angled himself there on purpose.

Back to the street again for Musetta's entrance. We trembled for her, but she managed fantastically well, laughing outrageously as she descended the narrow steps, carrying the Peke that

131

must weigh a ton. We four went off into the wings. Wendy Fine seemed to be going well. Someone reported in an awed undertone that she actually got one of the billiard balls into a pocket. Much later I learnt this was fixed! There was a great burst of applause after her Waltz song.

We fought our way back onto the stage. John Wilding carried me down the steps. We reached our positions in the OP corner. The band and the soldiers came on. We were waving, dancing. The curtain fell.

We changed quickly, but there was a long interval. Back up to the stage for Act III. We crept into the Tavern in darkness. Plastic beakers and the wine had gone up a grade – vin rouge but no longer toujours. Wendy Fine arrived – she looked wonderful, but was obviously nervous. Her carafe of water was there, but no wine glass. I offered to find it – I crawled off into the darkness. People everywhere, but no stage management. At last I saw Peter, Stage Manager, and grabbed his arm. He promised to bring one. I didn't know if the curtain had gone up or not. It hadn't. Peter brought the missing wine glass. No Pauline. Nothing we can do. I said she left the dressing-room when I did. The curtain really has gone up and Act III is underway.

Pauline arrived, much dishevelled, through the front door of the Tavern. Apparently John Copley caught her and made her play the Tart in the Cart with a chorus man. She was greatly agitated, and didn't know if she's always got to do it or if some chorus lady was off. She had lost her shawl. Musetta sang, and we made our entrance into the snow – which, strangely, didn't seem to be falling. Back into the Tavern once more – a silent toast to Domingo waiting in the wings. Now we can really listen to the music and the singing. They came to the last duet – dutifully we nodded off and pretended to sleep.

Then there was a wild scrimmage as we changed back into our street clothes. We all crept out into the auditorium to watch Act IV, the house was packed. There wasn't a vacant seat, and there were people standing everywhere. I finally found a perch on a step.

Act IV had improved so much since I saw it at the beginning of last week, everyone was singing superbly. The fooling around at the beginning of the act is excellent – all four men play so well together. Domingo clowns in the pink bonnet, Thomas Allen as Schaunard does his ballet dance. Then Musetta rushed in with the ill tidings about Mimi. And at last Katia was there – Domingo arranged her golden hair on the pillows on the bed. They brought her the muff and she warmed her hands. "The swallow has returned to her nest." For the first time I heard Katia and Domingo singing full out. Katia is so young. With her final fit of coughing I started to cry. Domingo drew the curtain slowly, haltingly across the great studio window at the back of the stage, and as he came down the stairs towards the bed there was the last great cry, a sound of some wounded bereft wild animal. The unearthly heartbreak. The great red curtains fell.

Defying superstition, the First Night went even better than the dress rehearsal. The critics were practically universal in their praise, the reviews were rapturous. One headlined his notice "Glorious new 'Bohème' at Covent Garden." The other notices were as fulsome, with such leaders as "Not a Dry Eye" and "All This and Billiards Too." And there was plenty of praise for John Copley, who had masterminded and directed this marvellous production. When they were in the early stages of planning, Sir John Tooley, the then General Director of the Royal Opera House, had said to Copley, "Make it a good one, John. We want it to last three or four years." Who could possibly have guessed or foreseen it would be forty-one years before the final curtain fell on this historic and record-breaking production of "La Bohème?"

CHAPTER TEN

Other operas

1975

So I settled down to enjoy the other performances in that first run of "Bohème." Rumours ran round the Opera House, and reached our dressing room, that John Copley (who was a resident House producer at Covent Garden at the time) was going to do a new production of Gounod's "Faust." Then the glad news that he was going to use all the actors from "Bohème" reached us. Our excitement was scotched when the rumour changed to, "all the actors *except one!*" I always imagined the latter amendment was put about by Miss Chitty just to keep us all on our toes.

But in the event, we were all booked for "Faust." The production, designed by Desmond Healey, was to have a suitably Medieval look. I was to be a Flower-Seller. My costume consisted of a black felt cloche hat over a white wimple, a vast orange skirt over layers and layers of petticoats and a tight black bodice. I thought I looked like one of those Russian dolls you can screw in half.

I don't remember exactly when I began to

hear that "Faust," in the opera world, is thought to be an unlucky opera, the equivalent of the "Scottish Play" in the straight theatre. This production certainly seemed cursed from the outset. The money had been put up by an American Foundation, with the proviso that the bass, Norman Treigle, sang Mephistopheles. He turned up to the first rehearsal on crutches having, he said, injured his foot. Hardly a promising beginning. Throughout the run his voice varied wildly, not only from night to night, but scene to scene. He missed a number of rehearsals, giving his understudy, Richard Van Allan, a chance to soar. But Treigle, odd looking in his scarlet costume and tights, cocked hat topped with a quivering feather, never missed a performance. But those who knew about voices muttered that they didn't know what was going on. Later we heard that Norman Treigle had cancer. He died two months after that revival of "Faust" ended.

Kiri Te Kanawa sang Marguerite, looking rather strange in the traditional blonde wig with pigtails. My great moment with her came in the Kermesse, the big market scene. She had to come to my flower basket, slung round my neck like an usherette's ice cream tray, and choose a single marguerite. Kiri seemed to find this seemingly simple task puzzling (but she was singing the leading rôle, and she didn't know it all that well.) To assist her, I cleared all the other flowers to the side of the tray, leaving the marguerite in single state dead centre. Even so, every evening there was a long pause while her fingers hovered uncertainly, and she said in her thick New Zealand accent and voice that reached several rows back in the stalls. "Which one?" "That one" – I would point soundlessly. Faust himself was sung by the chubby middle-aged Stuart Burrows. He looked like a Woolworth's reproduction of "The Laughing Cavalier." He always seemed robustly cheerful and good-humoured. When, and it happened fairly frequently, he missed his high note at the end of his aria in the Garden Scene, he giggled endearingly.

Quite early in rehearsals I heard that the Angels (who take Marguerite up to Heaven) were going to fly, or rather be flown. Ever since missing out on playing Wendy in Peter Pan (I always had too much bosom – anything even faintly sexy is verboten for that production) it'd been my ambition. So I got quite excited. Alas, it seemed the Angels were to be members of the Opera-Ballet. But one actress was needed, to cover for Kiri, who was far too valuable to fly. Alas, Kiri is very tall so I wasn't even in the running to be her double. Jo Douglas, one of the Elegant Ladies in "Bohème", got the job, but then reneged, pleading fear of flying. So the job finally went to a lofty chorus lady.

For this production we shared the big dressing room at the very top of the old building with the girls of the Opera-Ballet. I arrived for the first night to find them all sprawled about half-dressed except for their six-foot wings. They were all more than half-seas-over. Leslie Edwards (character dancer and pillar of the Royal Ballet,) had given each of them a bottle of champagne. They all pleaded fear of flying and seemed unable to perform these rôles unless suitably fortified with alcohol. Most evenings their conversation ranged around their various abortions, and I felt it was extremely fortunate that there were no mishaps with the flying. One of the critics ended his notice by saying that, "the vision of the angels on a wobbly magic carpet misfired." Gounod said, of his method of composition, "God sends me down some of his angels and they whisper sweet melodies in my ear." Well, not the Royal Opera House angels.

I thought the dress rehearsal was a hoot from beginning to end. In the "Army's Return" my partner was the smallest man in the chorus. As the curtain rose the army were supposed to swarm up from the pit and fill the stage. Only one member of the chorus arrived and he was wearing a rather smart suit and collar and tie (apparently his cozzie wasn't ready.) From the stalls, John Copley clapped his hands and shouted in dismay. It seemed only one ladder had been put in place, there were meant to be three. Once this had been rectified, and the chorus were all on stage and singing lustily, Pauline and I launched ourselves into the darkness, like escapees from St. Dunstan's, and attempted to locate our "husbands." Easier said than done, as all the men were wearing knitted balaclavas that completely obscured their faces. I located a relatively short man, and did "loving reunion" business all up his left side so that he could keep an eye on the conductor with his right. But, "I'm not your husband," he hissed. "David's over there!" I found him, just in time to wave my flag gaily for the end of "Gloire Immortelle." The art of flag waving is something you learn very early on at Covent Garden – no one is allowed to make a mess of it, as Boris Johnson did at the close of the Chinese Olympics. The art is to keep the end of the wand moving in a figure of eight.

All my actor friends were statues in the Church scene – they had to make terrible gestures at Marguerite, as, losing her wits, she flitted between them. I went down into the wings to watch. There was no audience for this dress rehearsal – it was officially closed and the fiendish friends had, for once, been banished. I started giggling again when I heard Stella announce, over the tannoy, "Statues, you needn't wear your heads for this run-through."

Then we all trooped on again to swell the chorus for "The Death of Valentin." From the auditorium, John Copley suddenly started giving us whispered directions through a microphone. "Get ready to cross yourselves – he's going to die." We all knew the cue, but were so unnerved we all flopped to our knees. "Get up you nits, he isn't dead yet," roared John. I tried to control my giggling as six shaking chorus men tried to carry Thomas Allen off. I prayed for the curtain to come down – finally it did.

Valentin (Marguerite's brother) was sung by the wonderful Thomas Allen. Except that he didn't do too much singing in that "Faust." As I arrived for the first night a notice had been put up, "Mr. Allen will not be singing his aria ('Avant de quitter ces lieux') tonight." And so it continued – performance after performance and it was cut. I think I heard him sing it twice – we understood that lovely Tom wasn't well. None of us realised that it was the beginning of a really serious illness that took him out of the profession and laid him low for many months. Luckily, he finally made a good recovery and had a glorious career. But it was another instance of the bad luck that dogged our "Faust."

The final incident was really serious. Faust is a long opera and we were all in the House for the entire evening, though not, of course, on stage all the time. Penny Leatherbarrow and I arranged our own supper break so that we could go into the wings and watch different scenes. Peter Morrell, the Stage Manager, would say, "Is it sausages and chips or the mad scene tonight?"

But our favourite was the Garden scene. One night we were watching Anne Howells as Siebel – in love with Marguerite and looking like a Principal Boy in thigh length boots. She was singing her aria, and she went up to the Holy Water shrine at the back of the stage to get the flowers blessed which she was going to leave for Marguerite. Suddenly she gave an agonised cry and collapsed onto the stage. The orchestra stopped playing and the whole House held its breath and waited for her to get up again. She didn't. She didn't move and appeared doubled up with pain. The curtain came smartly down and Mephistopheles and Stuart Burrows, awaiting their respective entrances, rushed onto the stage. Penny and I just saw them lift the hapless Anne and bear her away before we beat a hasty retreat to the canteen for the longest supper break on record.

As we'd been watching, everyone wanted to know what we'd seen and there was general speculation about what would happen next. Some of the chorus even changed into their going-home clothes, believing the whole performance would be cancelled. It was only by hearsay the rest of the story reached us. Anne had injured the cartilage in her knee and, stripped of her costume, was rushed off to hospital in an ambulance. And the powers-that-be started telephoning frantically. And what luck they had – they discovered Silvia Baleani, due to take over Siebel the following week, was actually in her London hotel having dinner. A taxi quickly brought her to the Opera House, and she was shunted into Anne's costume and the curtain went up again on the Garden scene – to rapturous applause, in a little over one and half hours. For good measure, Stuart had been asked to give a reprise of his aria to start the performance off again. He missed the high note. And giggled.

At the last performance I heard one of the chorus ladies had slipped off the ramp and sprained her ankle, and would be off work for several months. It seems that Gounod's Faust is indeed an ill-fated opera. But how I'd enjoyed it!

I'm lying in bed tonight, it's a summer night, and the pain in my leg is God-awful. It's rigid in its metal encasement. I can't move it and I can't ease it. It's the stretching, making it grow to match the other one. Wonderfully clever the way Mr. Groom is doing it, but oh, the agony. Why did it have to shorten? I suppose I'll be glad eventually, should I ever get back to having a life again, to being an actress? Will it ever happen? Will I ever be free again? It's been two years now. It's a summer evening and I'm lying looking at the trees outside my window. What solace those trees give me – they may only be planes, despised by so many but they mean so much to me. Time and time again, I've saved them. Tenants in the lower flats always want them cut down and destroyed completely – saying they block the light. When the trees are threatened, I always send a swift letter to Westminster Council. Luckily all the trees in this road have protection orders on them.

And looking at "my" trees tonight, I had a comforting thought. I remembered a book I read when I was little (I taught myself to read, quite early.) And for a long time this was my favourite – it was the story of a little girl who made her home and lived in a tree. I made a vow that when I was grown up I'd live in a tree. And looking at my linden tree tonight, almost filling my window, I seem to have made that dream come true. Dreaming of trees makes me think of "L'Elisir d'Amore." Each of the great tenors at Covent Garden sang the famous aria "Una Furtiva Lagrima" under a great wonderful tree, with spreading branches. Or am I imagining that? Was it painted on the backcloth? What was it really like?

Pauline and I were very excited when John Copley, who was a House director at this time, asked us, together with two other actresses, to be in his new production of "L'Elisir d'Amore." "I've got lots for you to do darling," he said, greeting me with his usual smacking kiss at the first rehearsal. And so it proved. Quite early on we started rehearsing the Giannetta Girls' scene. Giannetta, the young peasant girl, was sung by Lillian Watson and her "friends" were the youngest girls from the chorus. We rehearsed this scene in the beautiful Crush Bar, cramped, but steeped in operatic history. Before rehearsals even began we'd been given an introductory talk by Graziella Sciutti, a famous Adina from La Scala, Milan, who assisted John on the production. She entreated us all to act in the opera as if "the sun was shining out of our souls." I always tried to do this. L'Elisir was all such fun, it wasn't difficult.

Our Adina was the Japanese soprano Yasuko Hayashi, who always seemed to me at odds with the production, an unlikely Italian landowner. Nemorino, the poor peasant boy who is in love with her, was sung by the wonderful José Carreras. In one scene I had to run round the line of girls and go down on my knees in front of him on his "adesso," beseeching him to choose me for the first dance. Carreras was always so sweet about this. When the opera was revived, and the great (in every sense – voice and girth) Pavarotti sang Nemorino, I had to plead with the chorus girls to squeeze up together, so that with my run I could arrive back on cue. Pavarotti's huge size lengthened the distance I had to cover considerably. Then I had to jump up on "éredita," with excitement – when the girls hear Nemorino has inherited a fortune. Lillian Watson would clap her hands over my mouth to silence me, and generally got a laugh.

Beni Montresor had designed a delightful "twopence-coloured" toy theatre set for the opera. Our costumes were multi-coloured pinks and yellows and greens, full-skirted with tight bodices. Most flattering. During the overture, the chorus, as harvesters, came on and picnicked in the cornfield. We four actresses followed them on, with baskets of washing, which we mimed enthusiastically in the mill stream (complete with water wheel) at the back of the stage. In the revival with Pavarotti, we watched with fascination as the black dye trickled down his neck from his burnt-cork coloured hair. At one performance he brought a glass tankard of water onto the stage – for little sips, I thought. (All the principals have their dressers standing by with glasses of water. Singing is dry and exhausting work.) But we watched with fascination as Pavarotti dunked two fingers in the water and then stuck them up his nose, inhaling deeply. And all this on stage, while the opera was going on. Then he spat it out – straight down the front of Pauline's dress – she wasn't pleased. I was speechless with astonishment. We presumed he did it to clear his sinuses, and produce those beautiful notes and clear ringing tone which wowed the world.

We also learnt that the great tenor was very

superstitious. We often saw members of his huge entourage throwing nails and screws about on the path he would take from his dressing room to the stage. Apparently, if he found one before his first entrance, it put him in good humour and he was convinced it would be a 'good' performance.

In the wedding scene, Pauline and I had to carry on model geese. They were a wedding present from the villagers to Adina and Belcore – the Recruiting Sergeant she promised to marry. (Tom Allen was very uneasy in the part, and never sang it again after that first run.) The geese, who we christened Dilly and Dally, were monsters, stuffed with concrete and roped together in pairs. We could hardly lift them and for our entrance we had to go down a crowded flight of steps, hampered by the ropes, which tripped everyone up, including Sir Geraint Evans, who played the Quack Doctor, Dulcamara. Once, I was sitting on the floor nursing my goose (where else to hold it?) and Stella said to me briskly, "That goose is not a baby, Pamela."

During rehearsals, John had great difficulty getting everyone to be lively enough for an Italian wedding. He kept saying, "Dears, it's not Cheltenham on a Sunday afternoon." Later he discovered a busker's band in Leicester Square and got permission from the Maestro to have them playing on stage throughout the scene. That livened things up.

Sir Geraint really came into his own in his first scene when he arrived in a cut-out coach with horses. At the end of his wonderful patter scene, we all had to rush to him and buy bottles of his, as we thought, "wonderful" elixir. These were Harpic bottles overpainted in blue. Then we danced about, holding them aloft excitedly. I reflected as I pranced around, that nowhere else on earth would I be paid £28 a week to dance about with an empty Harpic bottle! John was always very particular about us actually paying for them. One evening I gave Geraint a prop coin and he said "shit." When Prince Charles came to a performance, and visited Sir Geraint in his dressing room afterwards, apparently he asked about these bottles. The Knight showed him the ones stowed away in his cloak (these were over-painted gin bottles.) Charles asked if he could have one as a keepsake. Of course, Geraint handed it over, reminding him that it was a love potion. At this time there were strong rumours about his romance with Lady Diana Spencer. Daringly, Geraint added, "I hope it brings you luck, sir!" Later, when the engagement was announced, he sent the Prince a cheeky telegram saying, "I'm very glad the elixir of love has taken effect." He was very surprised to receive an answering telegram, "The elixir worked but it was rather slow to act."

One performance before the final scene I noticed the Knight fiddling with a little girl from the chorus. I thought, "Oh no," and kept an eye on her throughout the scene. When Sir Geraint got to his third chorus and climbed onto the stool, she went and stood right in front of him, staring up, eyes all innocence. And then, to my complete amazement, I realised she was unrolling his words on sheets of paper, down her front! Four performances on, I hadn't noticed. It's very cleverly done. Pauline had also seen. At the curtain call she whispered, "I wouldn't have liked to pay £200 for a seat to watch you and me miming words we didn't know." But I did know them.

Carreras was lovely. He was quite my favourite tenor. His voice always reminded me of a blackbird bursting into song. I would go down to the wings to listen to the famous aria "Una Furtiva Lagrima," which he sang under the great tree (or was it the tree of my imagination?) He was a lovely person, too, and talked to everyone. He was having an affair with Katia Ricciarelli. She watched each of his performances from the OP corner, more Teutonic and Wagnerian looking than ever, though of course she's actually Italian, in a huge brown tweed cloak. She must have made it big though, she had a 100 guinea crocodile handbag and Cartier rocks all over her fingers. Either she had a tic in her eye, or she winked at me – I didn't really think she could have remembered me from "Bohème?"

The first night of "L'Elisir d'Amore," 18th December, 1975, was a Royal Gala. I managed to slip out front to admire the flowers and decorations – all up the Grand Staircase and in the auditorium. The Royal party were going to sit in the centre of the dress circle, not the Royal Box. This section was fenced off and decorated with swags of flowers and greenery and ribbons. The Queen Mother, all in white and dripping diamonds, came with Prince Charles, Princess Alexandra and the Hon. Angus

Ogilvy. The opera got off to a rather shaky start, but Sir Geraint pulled it all together and everyone got better. He came on in the Coach Scene and with his great patter song "Udite, O Rustici," delivered with his purple cloak billowing out behind him. At the end of the opera, as Pauline and I tottered down stage to wave our flags and take the curtain call, she whispered to me, "Perhaps next time round you and me'll get A VOICE…"

The season Pavarotti sang Nemorino, there was another Royal Gala to raise money for The Opera House itself. It was in dire financial difficulties at the time – (12 March, 1990.) Queen Elizabeth, the Queen Mother, came at least pretending to love every minute and dispensing her wonderful charm to everyone concerned. She brought Princess Margaret with her – who, when greeted by the Intendant of the time, Jeremy Isaacs, apparently retorted, "I hate opera." We heard that she spent the whole of Act II in the Royal Box ante-room, chatting to Norman St. John-Stevas, smoking and sipping whisky. I managed to change very quickly at the end and slipped out onto the street to watch them leaving in the royal car. The Queen Mother, ever smiling, her diamonds sparkling, was wearing a sea-green silk dress under her white fox stole. Princess Margaret, lost in the shadows of the farther corner of the car was still, as far as I could see, looking glum. The car drew silently away from the kerb, the Queen Mum still waving one white-gloved hand.

It seemed I had made a little success, insofar

as an actress can in an opera. Opera is about singers. It is the Great Singers audiences pay to hear. Actors and actresses merely provide the background to the scenes. On the last night Carreras came up to me in the wings and said jokingly, "Signora, you are to blame for everything that goes wrong in this theatre!" and went away. Then Lillian Watson came and tapped me smartly on the wrist with her fan. "You do realise you're the most unpopular person in this theatre, don't you?" And finally, Tom Allen who said, "Do *behave* yourself." Oh, it had all been such fun and such a lovely cast.

CHAPTER ELEVEN

Die Zauberflöte and other operas

1977

And tonight, on the radio, through the darkness and the pain, came "Die Zauberflöte." "The Magic Flute." *My* opera. Enraptured, forgetting everything, I listened to the overture that tells of the magic doors that will open. They will. They will. And later the great cry "Sie lebt! Sie lebt!" I will walk again. I will…

Mozart has always been my favourite composer since I discovered his music all those years ago when I was an A.S.M. Ken Tynan had chosen the Overture to "The Marriage of Figaro" as incidental music to his production of Garrick's version of "The Taming of the Shrew." I was in charge of the Panatrope, and playing those 33⅓ records opened up a whole new world for me that would eventually lead to the Royal Opera House.

Early in the New Year 1979, I was invited by the Royal Opera House to audition for the new production of "Die Zauberflöte." It was to be directed by August Everding, the Intendant of the Bavarian State Opera in Munich, where he had already done a production of "The Magic Flute." We were to be the wild animals Tamino tames during his aria "Wie stark ist nicht dein Zauberton," (to help remember this I translated it as "We're stark naked here in Surbiton.") I wondered what animal I could possibly be? I looked the score up in the library and it said, "He takes his flute and plays. All sorts of wild animals come and listen to him."

The audition was held in the studio at 45 Floral Street. This was immediately opposite the stage door, where many of the ROH offices were. I arrived in plenty of time, suitably attired in trousers and sweater. Quite a lot of the actors and actresses attended. Pauline hadn't been asked.

Then the audition started. We were told we were to be monkeys. I was thunderstruck, and really didn't know what to do. I went down on all fours and took a few lolloping steps. Then I rose up to beat my chest, and for good measure picked a few fleas. Soon it was all over. We were told to go outside the door while the powers-that-be considered their verdict.

When we went back in, I sat at the back of the room, sure that I hadn't got it. I was reprimanded by Stella and told to come nearer the front. The list was read out. Two bears, two monkeys, a gorilla, and a baby monkey – Pamela Binns. I was too surprised to take it in. That weekend I went to the zoo and studied monkey movements.

On Saturday, January 6th I was bidden to the theatre by a letter from the stage management assuring me it would be 'valuable' and 'beneficial' for 'slaves' and 'animals' to watch the Munich videotape recording of "The Flute." Purely voluntary, of course, but we all know what that means. ("If you happen to be passing Artillery Buggins, John Copley will be delighted to see you," etc.) The really keen turned up. We pinched chairs from the canteen, and sat in the ballet rehearsal room, about 20 yards back from the 15" screen, which proved to be in foggy black and white. Wayne (stage management) was there, mit score but also to supervise us. (What did they think we might do?) The lights went out. Hilde (German coach) asked for a torch. I scrabbled for mine (little Girl Guide that I am) and it was passed along the line. There were now about eight of us watching. Then the lights went on again. Wayne said ice creams and chocolates would be served in the interval. The film started again. There was a UFO hovering about the screen. This turned out to be the dragon. All the figures were about half an inch high. It is a very long opera. Pamina's dress must be white, she's always just a pale splash. The sound was not too good. My very musical friend, John Herrington, now playing one of the German-speaking Slaves, was trying to put his hands over his ears, but not to be seen doing it. The animals were coming on, we all leant forward, but it was difficult to make out anything at all.

At the next rehearsal, we had a run-through of our bits in the studio with Romayne, the Opera Ballet Mistress. Then we went into the auditorium to do the dance with Tamino. I was still bouncing on with the others on the opening two chords at this stage. We had hardly done this when Everding clapped his hands for us to stop. He came over to me and wagged a roguish finger. "You," he said, "You must not distract!" Dear Heavens – I haven't done anything – yet. My thighs were aching like hell, trying to keep down in the monkey position, and my legs had turned to jelly. Sandra was still yelling at me. (The girls are all real dancers.) At last we were allowed to go home. I drove Michael and Sandra to Embankment, and dropped Romayne in Northumberland Avenue. I was exhausted.

I spent the rest of the week alternately trying to break in my thigh muscle and cosseting the pain. I eventually decided a hot water bottle on each thigh eased the pain most. I recorded the aria on a cassette from a German radio broadcast. I played this every day, but could not remember where we galloped sideways, made funnels, etc.

A week later we had the second rehearsal at the London Opera Centre. Blizzard snow and ice made taking the car impossible. Miserable journey by District Line and bus. I walked about the east end of the Commercial Road a bit – it is a bleak, deserted moon-landscape under the snow. Eventually I plucked up courage to enter the London Opera Centre. The others were already there. As before, I was completely befogged by the dance, a fogginess that's going to continue for a long time to come, although Robin Leggate did it over and over again with us. He got very exhausted, and said he'd put on weight due to the meals at the London Opera

Centre (the canteen is very good.) He is flabby.

August Everding has departed – he's gone to look after his other "Flute" production in Rome. Christopher Renshaw, who has taken it over, is very sweet. He suggested I made a solo entrance from the OP corner to the flute music, after all the other animals have jumped on. He said, "Pamela, you will be all sweet and lovable and tiny and cuddly, won't you?" I nodded dumbly. I did my best at a monkey walk. Chris laughed and said it was like Kermit the Frog. Tobias – oh Heavens, I hadn't realised we were having him – he's Everding's personal assistant on this, and no one knows the ding-dongs we had over "Freischütz." No one else knows I even know him.

Anyway, he and Romayne became very severe and made me bend over. Both shook me and said how stiff my shoulders were, etc. Of course, I cannot explain about my plated leg. I was at last released. Long slow painful journey home, tubes crammed as there is a general train strike in the south east. Dragged myself up the hill and up the stairs. In bed that night I thought about offering my resignation, but decided to fight on a bit longer. We need the money, and the only other job on offer is cinema-usheretting in Muswell Hill.

Then we rehearsed on the stage for the first time. Romayne had promised me that we could have a run through in the ballet rehearsal room first but she refused, and we sat about aimlessly in the canteen. I produced a notebook and eventually, with great difficulty, got Terry John Bates to explain, and I wrote down the middle of the dance (I know first third and last third — it was this middle bit I couldn't fit into the aria at home.) At last I know I shall be able to learn it. The only way I can learn dances is to write them down and memorise. Then my brain knows and sends messages to my limbs. The dance went better.

The dress-rehearsal of "The Magic Flute". We wore our monkey skins for the first time. We wear leotards underneath them with padding on the stomach, thighs and knees. Mine is horrendously tight. Our dresser, Lynda, tried to stretch the garment over my knees and hips to give me some leeway. When I put the head on I couldn't see anything. I took the head off and cut away chunks of rubber with my nail scissors. At last I got the holes somewhere near my eye-line. Sandra came back from doubling up as the Queen of the Night — she goes up in the moon which is flown high above the stage, and looks fabulous.

The animal dance went surprisingly well, and we got applause (for the first and last time) and we were staggered. I met Michael Friend in the Nag's Head afterwards. He thinks the Coliseum production is better, including the animals. But he comforted me by saying we play the animals almost exactly as they probably were in Schikaneder's first production of the opera, i.e. very theatrically. We agreed that Ileana Cotrubas and Zdzislawa Donat as Pamina and the Queen of the Night sang divinely. Nor could Michael fault Thomas Allen's Papageno.

At last it was the first night of "Die Zauberflöte" – Thursday, February 15th, 1979. M. said Colin Davis (conductor) was on the radio at five to eight. I said, "What, the religious spot?" "No, but he was bubbling with enthusiasm about the company, saying all but two" (Ileana C and Miss Donat) "were home grown, and everyone was so young and enthusiastic."

The weather is dreadful – deep snow. I went down in the morning and dug out the car and unfroze the doors with hot water bottles. Came in frozen and tried to warm up my legs and go through the dance. During the afternoon, a blizzard blew up. Realised I couldn't take the car. Left home at 5pm and eventually got the train to Earls Court. From there – finally – to Covent Garden. I have never been so nervous in this theatre. I was absolutely pea-green petrified. I went up to the OP corner to watch the beginning of the opera. Wonderful overture. Tamino (Robert Leggate) going very well, being chased by the dragon (Terry John Bates.) The Three Ladies (Lorna Haywood, Ann Murray and Elizabeth Bainbridge) sang very well, and were very funny in their helmets and breastplates. When Papageno came on it was time to go down and dress.

Lynda helped me into the hated monkey skin. I went down to the OP corner feeling sick. Peter Morrell wished me luck. John Herrington (waiting to be a Slave) was in the corner. Silently, he pressed my hand. Speaker's scene seemed like it was never going to end. Cue came at last. There's the flute music. I'm a lost little monkey. Oh God, it seemed the longest loneliest walk in the world across the front of that stage. Dance didn't go well, it didn't seem to "gel." At the end I have to take the She-Bear's arm and Michael and I were late off. No applause. Learnt afterwards Lionel had been upset by a stagehand just before he went on. He wears the "Siegfried" bear-skin, which is too large and out of place, but this stage-hand said he looked shitting awful. Afterwards, Romayne had given us three bottles of beautiful white wine, Carolyn got paper cups and we sat around drinking. But we were all very depressed, and it was about as merry as a wake. Over the tannoy we heard lovely singing from Robin Leggate, Thomas Allen and Ileana Cotrubas. The rest of the opera seemed to be going very well.

We dressed in our monkey suits and went down for our final entrance as the curtain fell on Act II. Papageno and Papagena's (Lillian Watson) duet and the tiny children brought the house down. There was enormous applause at the end, which we could still hear as were undressing. Long, dispiriting journey home. I walked to Holborn Station, black ice everywhere and roads and pavements deserted.

Before our next performance I saw Romayne for the first time since the first night. I muttered something about the dance not having gone very well. She said she thought it did go well and added, "And Pamela, your entrance was marvellous, it was lovely. You completely convinced me you'd come down a palm tree and lost the other animals and your bearings." (I had, I had, I went off the music.) "You moved your head about like this" (she demonstrated) "it was sweet." Tonight was a broadcast, everyone sang very well.

In one of the revivals of "Die Zauberflöte" at Covent Garden, when a German tenor was singing Tamino, he forgot to bring his flute on for the aria "Wie stark ist nicht..." When he realised he let out a number of German expletives, and then he went down to the footlights (only there aren't any at Covent Garden) and sang his aria straight out to the audience. We were left stranded mid-stage, feeling very silly. We all hopped about a bit, praying for our cue to exit, which seemed an awfully long time in coming.

I am perpetually intrigued by the use of the number three in "The Magic Flute." My lucky number. It continues to haunt me – three chords to open the overture in this part-opera part-panto. Then three Ladies and three Boys. There is Osiris, Reason, married to Isis, Nature, both Egyptian gods, followed by Wisdom. Three again. And Tamino is subjected to three trials, overseen by three Priests. We all know Mozart was a Mason, and apparently the number three plays a large part in Masonic ritual.

But it didn't turn out to be a lucky number for the composer. He was desperate for money when he wrote "Die Zauberflöte" (hastily, for the downtown actor-manager Schikaneder, who also wrote the libretto and played Papageno.) His wife was ill and was taking the cure at Baden. Tragically, Mozart died in December, just two months after the first performance in September 1791. His seven year old son did attend the first night. How he must have loved Papageno and the animals.

I was always struck that it is Pamina who leads Tamino into the trials of Fire and Water. (Very poorly staged in the Covent Garden production.) And I can't imagine any more beautiful tune than when Pamina gives Tamino the flute. In the part Ileana Cotrubas is so lovely, intelligent, touching and musical. Robin Leggate made her a good partner as Tamino, and he was always helpful in the animals' scene, when he tamed us. I thought Thomas Allen was <u>wonderful</u> as Papageno, but the critics were lukewarm about his performance. Neither did they care very much for Lillian Watson's Papagena. I judged her first rate, especially in her first appearance as the old crone. Their final "Pa-pa-pa-pa-ageno" duet with the tiny children always brought the house down.

Sir Colin Davis conducted these first performances. Once, in South Korea, I'd been lucky enough to sit next to him for breakfast. I knew that he had once said, "Mozart is able to convince us all that we are acceptable people. We dance out of the theatre."

But my favourite scene of all is the Priests' at the beginning of Act II. Every night I go down and listen to the wonderful solemn music of Isis and Osiris. Robert Lloyd's Sarastro is magnificent. (In this act, Sarastro, having been a villain, becomes a friend.) The Priests are dressed as 18th century

Philosophers. Many of my friends are in this scene – Robert Lankasheer has a couple of lines to speak (in German) and Michael Reeves breaks my heart representing the new recruit in the Temple. George Bernard Shaw said all the religion he would need was in the music of Act II.

"Bohème" went on and on, but apart from that (and how welcome it was) the last really new opera production I was in was Giordano's contorted masterpiece "Fedora." My dear friend John Newbury and I considered ourselves very lucky to be chosen for the two main acting parts. I was to be the old Nanny/Companion to the leading soprano. And John was to be her Manservant. When I heard that the cast was to be headed by Mirella Freni I was overjoyed. I'd thought she was the perfect Mimi, and she'd been a heroine of mine for years. The plot of "Fedora" is so complicated it defies the most ardent Christie fans. In almost every scene there are secret agents swapping dark secrets, and undercover police scudding everywhere; and Nihilists – what exactly are Nihilists? And my beloved Carreras was in it (gravely thanking me when I congratulated him on his wondrous comeback after leukaemia. But the voice was never the same.) He played the Hero, of course, but was he a Baddie? Someone played the grand piano in Act I – the famous Intermezzo – and there was a Soirée.

For the final scene of the opera, Carreras and Mirella are on stage together, the scene is a chalet high up in the Alps. One of them is dying of poison, then the other commits suicide. I can't remember which did which, but it was all incredibly moving. John and I were behind them, there was no one else on stage. The singing was exquisite, but as their deaths approached a chorister in the wings took up a Swiss Yodelling song. John and I flopped to our knees, tears streaming down our faces at every performance.

When "Fedora" was revived the following year, both John and I got the sack. Naturally, we were both very upset. It seemed a lady in the Chorus had complained about me, saying the Opera House were wasting money on my salary, when one of them could do my part. (The Chorus were strangely unoccupied at the time.) Unfortunately, this dame got her wicked way and one of them (not the one who'd complained, thank goodness) replaced me and clambered into the elaborate velvet gown and donned the hat with the silver filigree brim that Freni had insisted was worn turned up. (And she knew – she'd done the production previously in Italy.) John's removal was far more mysterious and unaccountable. He was simply replaced by Michael Reeves. Just like that, with no explanations given. They are both very good actors, both absolutely right for the part. There was nothing to choose between them. Of course John was terribly upset and his removal seemed so strange, it was difficult to know what to say to comfort him. But at least we'd both been in the very first run of "Fedora" at Covent Garden.

By the time John Copley ceased to be a House Producer at Covent Garden, I was sufficiently "in" with the stage manager, Stella Chitty, for her to recommend me for parts and auditions. One day she called me aside and told me that the great opera director, Götz Friedrich was coming, from behind the Iron Curtain, to direct Der Freischütz at Covent Garden. I'd vaguely heard of Friedrich. I knew he was considered the Guru of opera production in Eastern Europe, and people went to kneel at his feet and learn from him. One particularly keen actress from Covent Garden had even made the pilgrimage. About Der Freischütz I knew nothing. I learnt that it was by Carl Maria von Weber, a thrilling story about young love blighted by failure in a shooting contest, that led to entanglement with the Devil himself, and there was a lot of spooky goings-on and spells and enchantment, until everything was righted by the appearance of a Hermit, who no one had ever seen before, and who arrives in the opera as a Deus ex Machina to ensure a happy ending. There was also a great deal of beautiful music. Stella said she was putting me forward for the part of "the Mother". "And remember Pamela –" she wagged an admonishing finger. "Götz loves smiling faces."

For reasons only known to the management, the auditions were held in the Central Hall, Westminster. I dressed carefully for the occasion – it was the era of the midi, I put on a soft wool pink and grey skirt, atop black patent boots that I hoped looked faintly Germanic. I didn't know where the Central Hall was, so after arriving at Victoria I asked a traffic warden. She looked me up and down before saying, "Nice. Is there a show on there?" Then she gave me directions. When it was my turn to audition, I advanced slowly to the centre of the tiny stage, my mouth frozen in a Rictus grin. I beat my chest like a mountain gorilla and announced "Die Mutter!" That was a fatal mistake, because from then on Götz thought I spoke German, which of course I don't, despite having studied it for a year at that seminary I was despatched to after my mother's affair with the Bishop.

That first year, I played three different parts. As well as The Ghost of the Tenor's Mother, I was a Carolean Court Lady in the final act, and a jolly peasant in Act I. For several weeks I enjoyed rehearsing Act I, there was clog dancing and much clinking of beer steins. My appearance in The Wolf's Glen wasn't mentioned, although Stella had given me the music and the libretto, which of course I'd learnt.

Then one bitterly cold January day, when I was clunking away happily on the stage at Covent Garden, I was told I had a private call with Götz Friedrich down at the Opera Centre that afternoon. There was no chance of going home to collect the Mini, so it was a long cold journey on the Underground to Aldgate East. At the Opera Centre I was shown into a bleak studio where Götz was holding forth to his entourage. Of course I didn't understand a word, and as my entrance was ignored, I huddled in a corner and tried to pretend I wasn't there. After what seemed like hours, Götz clapped his hands and uttered the magic words,

"Die Mutter!" I sprang to attention. A rug was laid on the floor, and the great director proceeded to give a demonstration of reeling and writhing. It seemed to go on for an awfully long time. At last he got up – he was a very tall man, he loomed over me and said, "Vell?" He pointed to the rug. Clearly it was my turn.

I knew I was to rise from the grave and signal to my son, Max, who was being inveigled by the wicked Caspar to take the magic bullets (which were cooking in a frying pan) and quit The Wolf's glen for ever. I took a deep breath and managed to stammer, "But it's only eighteen bars..." There was a terrifying silence. And at last Götz said, unbelieving, "Ze only eighteen bars?" Then he demanded to see the score – no one had a copy. Another horrifying wait until one was produced. He grabbed it, found the place, and studied. He must have verified my words, because he suddenly turned his back and there was a torrent of German I didn't understand. His henchman, Tobias, stepped forward. "Just do what you can, Pamela," he said, and I was dismissed. Götz never spoke to me again.

So I continued to practise my "Flee the Glen" mime, realising I had to be very quick. I was to wear a white shroud, and a cap that covered my head, complete with a strap to support my chin. Even Robert, the head of make-up at Covent Garden, approved of what I did; I put green under the white of my face, to give it a mouldy-in-death look. My eyes were hollowed out in dark grey to make them look like sockets, and of course I made up my hands. But friends who came to performances reported that all they could see was the fluttering of a very small hand.

Once we were performing, Stella, in the silver slippers she habitually wore, and armed with a torch, would take my hand and lead me onto the darkened stage, where the Wolf's Glen was being set. We picked our way between the polystyrene boulders that were being arranged. They would roll about realistically with the thunder that marked the climax and the end of the scene. I would lower myself carefully into the deep grave cavity, and after ascertaining that I was all right, Stella would snap off her torch and leave me to it. One night, after she'd gone, and I thought the curtain was going up any minute, one of the stage hands who'd been arranging the boulders, launched himself into the grave on top of me. "I want you! I want you!" he hissed. He was very, very drunk. Hardly able to breathe for the beer fumes, I said primly, "Get off me at once. You're ruining my make-up!"

Another character in the scene is the Devil, called Samuel, and he was played by a wonderful old singer, Forbes Robertson. Every night he would cheerily call down into my grave, "You all reet, Missus?" He couldn't understand why the young singers at Covent Garden were afraid of forgetting their lines. (The central prompt box had recently been banished.) "All yer 'ave to do is make up any old sounds till yer get back on yer music. "Ere —" he gave a scornful nod in the direction of the audiences, "They won't notice a thing…"

Once The Wolf's Glen was over, I'd remove all my "dead" make-up, and substitute a straight one to be the Court Lady in the last act. Originally for this I was given a most flattering "bubbles" wig. Even an actor who'd never been over-friendly admitted, "Pamela, that wig takes years off you. You should get one like it." By the opening night a much plainer one had been substituted. But I still had the most flattering velvet hat with a long curling drooping feather, matched by a beautiful cozzie.

Much of the music of "Der Freischütz" was lovely. Lucia Popp gave a beautiful performance as Agathe, though she had trouble with the spoken dialogue. I often saw her pacing the corridors of the Opera House, defiantly muttering the lines to herself. But the most haunting melody of all was The Bridesmaid's Song, movingly sung by six members of the Chorus as they wound their way through the forest, taking the ill-fated Bridal Wreath to Agathe.

CHAPTER TWELVE

I took my washing to the Kabuki

1979

In September 1979 the Royal Opera House Company were going on a Far Eastern tour. They were going to Seoul in South Korea; and Tokyo, Yokohama and Osaka in Japan. I was asked to join the company, as one of the operas they were taking was "Die Zauberflöte" and I should be needed for the monkey dance. They were also taking "Peter Grimes," which I wasn't in, and "Tosca." I was hastily co-opted as a nun in Act I of the latter. It was all very exciting. The whole of the Covent Garden orchestra were going, as well as the chorus and the principals.

We were given little red books to guide us, which included such helpful hints as "The Second World War is not a recommended subject for conversation in Japan." For the flight out we had to be at the Royal Opera House by 5.00am. Our visas had been got for us, and we'd had all the vaccinations. As the first Underground train was 5.47am, I got a minicab, which arrived at 3.50am taking me completely by surprise. But I was at the

Opera House soon after 4.00am. We had coffee and biscuits, and then climbed into the coaches that were waiting in Bow Street. I was in the first one to leave at 4.30am, sitting behind the two old Johns (actors.) Sergeant Martin, the Head Doorman, stood in the road with his topper on, and saluted us off. It was still dark, and we wound our way through dreary South London. It took over an hour to reach Gatwick. In the duty free I bought two small bottles of whisky and a Ma Griffe atomiser. John Tooley was there to see us off, talking to the press etc, but apparently not coming with us. The tour was led by Paul Findlay, his assistant. In the end I was among the last to board the jumbo jet. Of course I couldn't find my seat, but Peter Morrell (stage manager) leapt up and kissed me. Eventually settled next to stage staff electrician and Anna Cooper (chorus.) Our take off was delayed because of mist. We finally left Gatwick at 8.00am.

Two very shy little Japanese hostesses in navy dresses and red aprons with daisies on them demonstrated yellow life jackets. They did this in Japanese and there was a dreadful American commentary which nearly brought the house/plane down, it seemed so obscene when they inflated the life jackets. They got cheers and cat calls from the company. A nippy little Japanese steward in a navy suit and bow tie rushed up and down the aisle saying, "Please do not laugh, please take seriously." Kenton (actor) sitting behind me, (we're all in the middle block) explained to him that it was only the American commentary we found funny. The two

Japanese hostesses disappeared in blushing confusion. More screams of laughter when boiling hot face flannels were brought round for us to wipe our hands on. Frankly no one knew what to do with them at first. Then breakfast was served – grapefruit, hot scrambled eggs, bacon and sausage. I only ate the eggs. Two different rolls, butter and marmalade, and two cups of coffee. I took my malaria pill. Discovered I should have been given streptomycin tablets, and hadn't got them. One of the orchestra took all his malaria tablets in one go.

We flew over Greenland, which was brown, like fruit cake with icing. I saw a magnificent crater, snow ringed. As we were going to fly over the North Pole I had taken a small compass with me. I hoped that going over the Pole it would whizz round and round, but in the event it didn't move at all.

Our first stop in the twenty-five hour flight was Anchorage in Alaska. We landed at 6.10pm (their time, we had to put our watches on two hours.) Mount McKinley peaked bright pink in the morning sun as we flew over it. In the terminal there was a huge stuffed polar bear standing on its hind legs, fully ten foot high. We were all photographed beside it. Then on to Tokyo. Everyone tried to sleep.

We arrived at Narita Airport and transferred to a Japan Airline flight to South Korea. We touched down at Kimpo Airport, Seoul, at twelve midday. It took an age for us all to get through immigration. Inadvertently I stepped over the red line, and a soldier rushed at me, his gun at the ready. We were directed to waiting coaches, and then sat for hours in the blazing sun. I had never felt anything like it, I thought I was going to pass out with heat stroke. Eventually we set off in a motorcade, with screeching police motorcycles beside us.

At last we reached the Lotte Hotel, the biggest hotel I'd ever seen. (The room rate was 52 dollars a day.) I was lucky enough to have a room to myself, on the eleventh floor. (Most people had to share, but as there were five actresses on the tour it was an odd number.) Unfortunately my room faced towards the North Korean border, and there was special frosted glass in the window so that you couldn't see out. There were other signs of military activity: one night when I was trying to get to sleep all the lights in the room suddenly came on, and I found I couldn't switch them off. I went to the other actresses' room across the corridor. It faced the other way, and they had ordinary glass in their window. We watched lines of tanks rumble past on their way to the North/South Korean border.

We had a free day, and we all visited a Korean village. It was a bit of a disappointment – like an al fresco Ideal Home. There was one solitary cow on show, and umpteen farmers' traditional thatched wooden houses that looked like hen coops. When I was staring blankly at one of these I heard a distant ranting and roaring. This turned out to be Robert Lankasheer, the oldest of the actors. He was shouting, "If I see one more wooden house I shall go mad!" I caught up with him and suggested we should go for a coffee and give

170

the seventeen other hen coops a miss. This was the start of our long friendship. I was especially glad of his companionship as, having fair hair, which is virtually unknown in Korea, wherever I went people wanted to touch me, which I found very unnerving. Some of the chorus bought Korean national costumes at the folk village. I wondered where they were going to wear them.

I loved being a nun, together with Jenny Thorne, in "Tosca." We scuttled on together in Act I, being careful to avoid Scarpia, as the great Te Deum was being sung. Colin Davis was the conductor. Cavaradossi was being sung by José Carreras, Tosca by Montserrat Caballé and Scarpia by Ingvar Wixell. It was all very exciting.

The opera season opened with "Tosca." Carreras had missed his plane, and the one after that was cancelled, and he only arrived at the last moment, so he was not in good voice. Everyone was very tense. President Park came to the performance. It was the wonderful old Zeffirelli production from Covent Garden, redirected for the tour by Ande Anderson.

Everyone told me about the fabulous market in Seoul and the wonderful bargains to be picked up there. Then one of the actors said there were puppies' and kittens' heads displayed on slabs, and I decided I must, at all costs, avoid going anywhere near the market. And, for the duration of my stay, I became a vegetarian. Sadly I didn't manage to keep it up afterwards.

One day, when I was out shopping alone, I

got completely lost in the maze of narrow crowded streets. Fearing that I might inadvertently come to the market, I panicked. Then I remembered the little red books we'd been given, filled with helpful hints on how to deal with such emergencies. I fished my copy out of my handbag, and, grabbing the nearest passer-by, pointed to the address of my hotel – clearly printed in the book. It didn't say anything about the sex of the person you should accost for help. The man I'd stopped, and his arm was already encircling my waist, couldn't believe his luck. Here was this blonde from the west clearly inviting him back to her hotel! Too late I realised my dreadful mistake. I was being expertly piloted through the thronging crowds – obviously to a fate worse than death. All seemed lost, but at that moment John Wilding, my lovely strong first partner from "Bohème," but also on this tour, rounded the corner. In a flash, he took in the situation. Immediately he linked his arm through mine, pulled me away, and we walked off as if we'd been engaged for years. Collapse of one poor little Korean man as his dreams evaporated. It was the last time I went shopping alone in Seoul.

It was the final night of the opera in Seoul, with "Die Zauberflöte." After the performance there was a presentation to Dr. Kim Sang Man who was chairman of the Dong-a Ilbo newspaper, which had invited the ROH to South Korea. He was accompanied by his wife, who wore pink national dress (it's rather like a Japanese kimono.) Sir John Tooley (who had flown out) gave him a score of

"Tosca." Surely records would have been more suitable? Sir John made a speech, about how honoured we all were, and then a man from the British Council spoke. We were all grouped round on the stage, I'd taken off my mask. Chris Renshaw (director) said, "One small monkey clapping." But for a minute I really did feel very proud.

We had all collected our boarding passes for the flight to Tokyo. I got up early as our luggage had to be outside our doors at 8.00am. Then hung about after our last breakfast in the ballroom. The Hotel Lotte gave us a great send-off. They served tea and coffee, and all the women in the company were given a salmon pink rose-bud, and everyone had a box of petit-fours. When we got into the waiting coaches all the hotel staff were lined up in the underpass, and they clutched at our hands as we drove off for Kimpo Airport.

We boarded the plane, and there was a mix-up over seats. I got a window one, but trod on £13,000's worth of Strad violin trying to get to it. Luckily the violin was in its case and unhurt. We were an hour late taking off, but at 2.30pm we saw the green and white Korean hills for the last time. Then we flew through dense mist. But at last we emerged into blue sky and white fluffy clouds – as we were above these it seemed as if the plane was flying the wrong way up. Then the sea, looking like a vast mud flat. We flew all up Japan. I saw Mt. Fuji sticking up through the clouds like a Christmas pudding coming out of cream.

We were hours at Narita Airport, going

through customs and being searched, but at last we boarded buses. The drive into Tokyo took nearly two hours. For the first part the landscape looked like Surrey, then that gave way to factories and flyovers.

Finally arrived at the New Otani Hotel. After a group check-in in the lower lobby, I found I had a single room on the 14th floor. Oh the joy. The room was furnished in buff and orange, with a minute bathroom. The Japanese are very small, so everything is just the right height for me. In the dressing-table drawers there were grey and white kimonos to sleep in.

In the evening we had a full "Tosca" rehearsal at the NHK Hall where we were playing. We were taken and returned to our hotel by coach. Montserrat Caballé did not arrive, so after an hour the rehearsal was abandoned and the management tried to locate her. At last the telephone rang.

"Here is Montserrat Caballé. I am in my room at the hotel. For one hour and twenty minutes I drive round Tokyo in a taxi. Then I say to the driver, "Well, you no know NHK hall. You know Hotel Otani? Good, we go Otani." So here I am. What you want I do now?"

It was too late to go on with the rehearsal. Ruby (little old actress) and I got hysterical trying to find the canteen, but we did eventually, and had water ices. Back at the hotel I was whisked to the 22nd floor by mistake.

The hotel had a stern list of "Rules of Conduct" affixed to the bedroom door. These included; "Not to use the guest room for purposes other than sleeping, eating and drinking" and the contrary-wise; "Not to bring meals, drinks, foods or beverages into the hotel unless authorised;" "Not to use the guest room or hallway for cooking, ironing or heating;" "Not to bring items into the hotel such as animals and birds, offensive smelling items, illegally owned guns and swords, gasoline, explosives, inflammable items or bulky objects;" "Not to use the hotel for soliciting business of any type unless specially authorised;" "Not to make trouble or annoy guests by taking sleeping drug other medicines;" "Hotel will reject to accomade (sic) the guests when they have infectious disease" and so on for a further three pages.

Of course we did cook in our rooms. Storing melting butter among my sweaters was the least of my problems. John Wilding had given me a heating element for making mugs of instant coffee. It had to be plugged into the television socket, and took ages to warm the water. But food and drink were very expensive in the hotel.

The New Otani was set in luxurious grounds, which included a lake full of carp. These fish were huge, up to three foot long, and there were a few blue ones among the gold and silver. They threshed the water in an alarming fashion when they thought you were coming to feed them. There was piped Muzak bird-song throughout the garden. There was also an inter-denominational chapel which was advertised as being open twenty-four hours a day, but was always shut when I passed it.

Somehow I never managed to catch the Tuesday morning Religious Breakfast in the Rose Room either.

It was the first night of "Tosca." The Duke of Kent attended officially with the British Ambassador and his wife. I met Carreras in a lift at the hotel at lunchtime, and he said he was a bit throaty.

We had to make our own way to the theatre, and I set out with Bob. He shamelessly picked up a young Japanese man on the Underground, leaning over and saying, "May I ask how old you are?" But it worked, this youth directed us. Something went wrong with one bar of the music in Act I, and I heard Carreras, very excited, saying, "It was a cheat." I think the nuns went OK. Mary Morse-Boycott, Ruby, Sandra, Jenny and I watched the last two acts on a colour TV monitor in the Green Room. It was very exciting, though the chorus said unkindly that Caballé and Carreras look more like mother and son than lovers.

At the end of the opera there was a rapturous standing ovation. Caballé, Carreras and Wixell were presented with huge bouquets of dark red roses, which they finally threw to the orchestra, although Carreras didn't want to part with his.

We'd all been looking forward to visiting the legendary Kabuki Theatre in Tokyo. I'd been invited to join a group with Sir Geraint (who was playing Balstrode in "Grimes") and Lady Evans. The performance began at 11.30am and lasted exactly five hours and twenty minutes.

We paid ¥3,600 for our seats, they were at

the back of the stalls, but near the right hand sidewalk down which some of the actors made their entrances. All the parts are played by men. They do extraordinary gliding walks, especially the ones playing women who put in an extra kick to make their kimonos go sideways. The orchestra consisted of one man plucking a long white banjo, and one reciter – was this "thoughts" or recitative? Our hero was like a wrestler, very square and muscular in a black and white toga-looking garment hitched high. He took an age to die. Inside the theatre was painted brownish-red, and decorated with scarlet lanterns. Most of the ladies in the audience were in kimonos. During the interval people bought beautifully packaged meals in origami boxes.

The cherry blossom scenery was like a Southend pantomime, and there were chorus men in white with badly joined bald wigs. It was very exciting when a Guard came on right by us – he was a gigantic man in black and gold. The climax was a dance, evil spirits took over, huge and scarlet in buskins. The great green bell of the Monastery fell.

Kabuki audiences are like Italian opera ones, they know the piece by heart, and wait expectantly for a special line or a particularly telling piece of business. The plots are wildly complicated. Lady Evans was particularly good at unravelling ours, and she was always whispering to tell us what was going on. But Sir Geraint turned to me in the first interval and said, "It's Spike Milligan's picnic, isn't it?" After three hours he'd had enough, and left the theatre rather noisily. Lady Evans stayed to the bitter end with the rest of us.

I'd insisted on taking my laundry with me. I knew I wouldn't have time to return to collect it, and that during the evening performance I should get my only chance in the week to use the communal iron. I'd done the washing the previous evening, and now I'd packed everything into a large C&A carrier bag. My companions voiced their disapproval, but my laundry was safely stowed away under the seat before the performance began.

Late that night, after "Die Zauberflöte," I travelled back to the hotel with the basset horn player from the orchestra. The Underground was crowded, and we were strap-hanging. I can never do this in London, but everything in Japan is just the right height for me. My beautifully pressed laundry was neatly packed in the C&A bag which I was holding with extreme care. Suddenly, a seated Japanese gentleman lifted the bag from my hand in one neat movement. I let out a muffled scream, and the basset-horn player put his hand over my mouth. But I didn't care if it did create an international incident. My precious laundry had been stolen, including the dress in which I intended to travel home. The basset horn player stopped me from screaming again. "Don't ..." he whispered, "he's only being polite." "Polite my foot," I said, "it's *my* washing." "No, it's Japanese good manners. He's sitting, you're standing. He's going to hold it until you reach your station." Suppressing thoughts that it would have been politer to give me his seat, I kept an eagle-eye on my precious carrier for the remainder of the journey. But my companion was right, when we arrived at Akasaka-Mitsuke, the stranger returned my laundry with a polite bow. I snatched it back with a muttered, "Arigato" (thank you.) Widow Twankey was in business again.

The Company were to do one performance in Osaka. We flew from Haneda Airport, taking overnight bags with us. (Our luggage would follow.) We flew in a jumbo jet that not only took all 350 of us, but Japanese passengers as well.

The Royal Hotel turned out to be even grander than the New Otani. Much to the envy of the other actresses I had a single room again. It had Japanese rice-paper sliding shutters to the window, and a low table and chair, and pale green flocked wallpaper. In the bathroom there were lots of free goodies. In the foyer there was a real waterfall and a stream with live ducks on it. The brochure described it as "the watered garden, with triple cascades, quite unique and particular in its thought, construction, presents a refreshing impression to lounge guests, mornings and evenings." The little boys who play the Genii in "The Magic Flute" said, "It's lovely. A baby fell in!" In the Royal you could go and fill your ice bucket at a machine in the corridor if you could find it in the maze of passageways.

While we were in Osaka, Montserrat organised and gave a concert at Hiroshima with Nina Walker as her accompanist. All the proceeds went to surviving Hiroshima victims.

Nearly the entire company went by coach to visit Kyoto, the ancient capital of Japan. We visited Kiyomizu (Clear Spring) Temple, perched on the edge of a sheer precipice so that the wooden beams of its foundations stretch right down the cliff face. I was so excited I nearly fell over, but was saved by Sir Geraint Evans clutching the belt of my coat just in time. At the very bottom, if you can face the climb, are three sacred springs. If you drink of them all I think you are promised a long life, happiness, and at least a hundred children. A few hardy members of the chorus made the long descent. Then we went to Sanjusangendo, with its Hall of a Thousand and One Kannon (the Buddhist personification of Mercy) each one of them individually carved. In the corridor behind the Hall there are twenty-eight extraordinary and exquisitely carved statues of the "Faithful Followers." They had an unforgettable combination of human and animal features.

Then we had a sit-down lunch, squatting on the floor on cushions, five or six of us round each burner, while one of the party prepared our egg and fish and seaweed. Sir Geraint hated it even more than I did, and, like me, he was unable to use chopsticks. Finally he gave up the struggle and said, "Feed me, Brenda," and Lady Evans popped food into his mouth like a baby bird.

After lunch we went to see the Silver Pavilion, Ginkaku-ji, though down the centuries no one has actually got round to facing it with the precious metal. In the grounds there is a huge and carefully shaped mound of grey gravel, the top rounded off to form a perfect concave. Here, the leaflet assures you, "The Emperor was frequently enjoyed (sic) while watching the moon."

Then we went to see the Golden Temple, or rather a replica of it, for the original was burnt down by a deranged young monk in 1954. (But we learnt that in Japan it is never advisable to ask how old anything is, buildings have constantly been destroyed by fire and wars, and they are always rebuilt.) The Golden Pavilion, built on stilts, seemed to hang serenely above the water surrounding it, with the Golden Phoenix crowning its pointed eaves. (I did ask a Japanese lady what kind of bird it was, and she promptly replied, "Is pigeon.") On the edges of the lake, little old lady gardeners grubbed for weeds, the large white brims of their bonnets almost obscuring their deeply lined faces. It was the most haunting experience.

We had a stage and orchestra rehearsal and a performance of "Die Zauberflöte" in the grandly name Festival Hall. Actually the theatre is too ghastly, you go in by the front of another hotel, through a door and down some stairs, and then through the hotel kitchen and across an underground car park, and finally up five flights of stairs to the dressing-rooms. Mary Morse and all the Papageno children (who are recruited locally) got stuck in the lift, and it was ages before they were rescued. Stuart Burrows sings Tamino, and Terry John Bates does the Serpent who threatens him. The three ladies are Helen Lawrence, Diana Montague and Elizabeth Bainbridge. The Queen of the Night is Barbara Carter. Papageno is Thomas Allen, and Papagena, Elaine Mary Hall. The Speaker is Ingvar Wixell, and Sarastro, Robert Lloyd. Alberto Remedios and Michael Burt are the Armoured Men.

When I finally got to the dressing-room Romayne said she'd seen Christopher Renshaw (director.) He'd said how good the animals had been all along, but he never saw us all together to tell us. But we met him after the dance tonight, on the endless stairs. He said, "I could swear all your faces actually move, you're so full of expression."

The theatre is so awful. Peter Morrell (stage manager) came up to our dressing-room and said we wouldn't be able to get round the back of the set, so we were to enter for the second part of the dance from the prompt side. He said, "How many of the animals weren't in our dressing-room?" I said, "The men." He said, "Tell all the tigers and lions and giraffes and whatever else we have in this travelling-circus!" The temperature soared to 86° and we all nearly died. We thought someone was having a shower in the next dressing-room, but it was the rain. Everyone said the typhoon was coming.

We didn't fly back to Tokyo until the evening so it seemed an endless day. I was sad to say "goodbye" to my little Japanese room. I had a window seat on the plane. There was a bejewelled view of Osaka as we took off. After that – darkness

– turbulent weather. The typhoon is coming. I got a bit nervous when the stewardesses suddenly stopped serving fruit juice in mid-flight.

Back at the New Otani I found I had a room to myself on the 12th floor. Changed very quickly into my Indian dress. Then there was a fabulous party in the hotel for the whole company given by the Japan Art Staff. The food was delicious; sliced almost raw roast beef, chips, chicken, lemon meringue pie and ice cream. Such a welcome change after sushi. On the tables there were beautiful flower arrangements and silver and huge chafing dishes. There were Japanese waiters and musicians. Bob Grey (an actor from "Grimes") processed round the room playing his bagpipes. Then we were all presented with medals. Paul Findlay made a speech and said he was very proud of us all.

We had another free day and I was able to go on a long sight-seeing expedition. We set off by coach at some unearthly hour of the morning. First we went to see the Great Buddha at Kamakura. The seated statue, forty-four feet high, has the most extraordinary aura of composure. At last we left this oasis of peace, and drove for miles beside the Pacific Ocean. (Bob teased us all by saying he saw penguins.) Then we reached Lake Hakone. After lunch we crossed the lake in a Mississippi-style steamer. Unfortunately, the weather had broken, it was pouring with rain and the tops of the mountains were hidden by clouds.

Then the coach climbed higher. We

stepped out into dense and swirling fog, not knowing what was going to happen next. Hardly before we realised it, Bob and I were pushed into a cable car, already crammed full with seven little Japanese gentlemen. We swung out into space. I just had one glimpse of bubbling bright yellow sulphur craters at the bottom of the ravine. Then the clouds closed in again. We returned to Tokyo by bullet train. Riding in it, you don't seem to be going so very fast – it is only when you notice the scenery whizzing past that you appreciate the train's tremendous speed. Mary Stevenson, of the chorus, tried to film one of the trains as it went through the station. She was using her husband's cine camera. She said," I don't think I got it – the wee red light was on. But I got the sound."

The Guide on the Hakone trip said the Japanese have discovered catfish can predict earthquakes – their whiskers droop down. This will be handy as Mary Morse-Boycott keeps some in the Earl's Court Road.

We visited many temples, including Asakusa-Kannon, one in the eastern part of Tokyo. We walked up a long cheap shopping arcade decorated with plastic flowers. I bought a blue patterned head scarf and a little black wooden cat. The big main temple is Buddhist, with a Shinto shrine to the left. Our guide told us to anoint our frail parts with the incense smoke billowing from a huge cauldron. Then we had our fortune told – you had to choose a little drawer to open. I got number 100 – this was very bad. I had to go and hang the piece of paper on a washing line to blow away the ill luck. On my second go I got "Little Good Luck, the moon is obscured by clouds. You are very kind to other people, and very decisive in making decisions." Bob pulled an awful face at that. He got "Very Big Good Luck" and was blessed by Buddha.

I tried again and again at all the other temples we visited, but always drew "Little Good Luck." The story of my life?

Our final performance in Japan was "Die Zauberflöte," very sad. The next day we were leaving for London. We had to put our suitcases outside our hotel bedrooms between 10.00am–noon. They were then collected and taken to Narita Airport and we followed at six o'clock in the evening. It had been a long day and then the two hours drive through landscape that strongly resembled Surrey. We, and our luggage, were thoroughly searched in a long wooden hut beside the motorway before we were even allowed into the heavily guarded airport. There were soldiers everywhere. There was a last, personal searching and x-raying of everything in the customs; and then it was Alaska, over the Pole, and home. Just before take-off the captain of the Jumbo jet wished us all "a pleasant fright." The Japanese "R's" are always surprising.

On the plane there was a spare seat next to me, and I was tucked up in a rug, so I managed to sleep for some of the night. As we came over the Hebrides, breakfast was served: it was sushi for one last time. How I longed for coffee and croissants. At 6.45am we landed at Gatwick Airport, only ten minutes late. But everybody had bought so much it took an age for the company to pass through customs. At midday, Bob and I were among the last to board a coach for the Royal Opera House. We arrived at last, and Forbes Robinson was kind enough to get me a taxi and load my luggage into it. Home at last, after the journey of a lifetime.

CHAPTER THIRTEEN

ESP: "There are more things in heaven and earth..."

Before time and later

Rehearsals for yet another "Bohème" started just after I returned from the tour. Everything seemed to be going well. John Copley was in his usually ebullient form. There was to be no General (or Dress Rehearsal) this time. We were going to open with a midday matinée performance for children.

We usually did at least one in each revival, and the kids always adored it – the curtain was left up so that they could see the scene change between Acts I and II – there were "Oohs" and "Ahs" as the Café Momus set glided majestically (sometimes) down to the footlights, with us all holding onto the wine bottles to prevent them falling off the tables. This glide down to the footlights only started after the mechanisation of the Opera House 2000–2002. Previously, the scene change had been done manually by a great army of stage hands – dexterously throwing looped ropes – and the flats, once secured, being literally lifted off the stage.

Stage Managers used to come from all over Europe to witness this feat, presided over by the indomitable Stella Chitty. And incredibly, this manual change was accomplished in less time than when it's done by all the computerised machinery.

The day before I'd had to have a back tooth extracted. It had taken a long struggle, and perhaps unwisely, my dentist kept topping up the local anaesthetic. I was almost in a coma when I left the surgery, and I've no idea how I got home. I fell into bed, and slept for twelve hours. When I woke I was still feeling peculiar, but managed to get to the theatre in time for this matinée.

I think I did everything I usually did in Act II. But when I was sitting in the Tavern in Act III – that's when things became really strange. I'd done my move out onto the stage and back into the tavern without mishap, and gradually I became aware of hundreds and hundreds of grey shapes – they were people, so many, yet not bunched together, each separate, and yet they were all one. And they weren't threatening or engulfing me, they were enjoying the music, as I was.

I looked round the table and Jenny and Pauline were whispering together – we had to keep quiet as we were on stage – but they hadn't noticed anything odd. They didn't seem to see the hundreds of grey and silver shapes that surrounded us, the souls of singers who'd thronged the stage in years gone by and were always there, only that day I was made aware of their presence and privileged to see them. I made my exit in the usual place –

Basil always helped me down the step, and I put on my street clothes and went home on the Underground. And as I turned into my road I wasn't at all surprised to see a coal cart, drawn by a Shire horse, and the driver, in Victorian clothes, delivering coal to one of the houses. I went upstairs and into my flat and lay on the bed. Almost immediately, Eileen came to me and was very comforting. Among many things she said it would be a long time before I came to join her. Then I fell asleep and by the next day, Sunday, everything was normal.

Things like this often happened when I was young, but when you're a child you just accept them. Time past and present; I'm never quite sure which is which. Parts of my Grandfather's house at Lichfield dated back to before the Civil War. The Close was fiercely Royalist, divided from the City which supported the Roundheads by the moat, parts of which still survived as the Minster Pool at the bottom of our garden. The oldest part of the house was a flight of twisting stone steps which led down into the garden. In 1940, shortly after the war had started, a hole appeared in the gravel path at the foot of the staircase. As children, we were thrilled, but we were kept well away from the gaping void. As the war was on, no one had the time, or money, to investigate, and it was unceremoniously filled in. But it was thought to be the entrance to the secret tunnel under the moat through which the Royalists had received supplies when the Close was besieged. A siege that ended in victory when a royalist sniper, perched on one of the Cathedral spires, shot and killed the commanding Roundhead General, Robert Greville, 2nd Baron Brooke, in the central square of the city.

The house entrance to the stairs was a thick oak door with heavy iron fittings. It was locked every evening. My mother had just done this one night, and I was watching her from further along the corridor, when behind her the door, creaking on its rusty hinges, slowly swung open. There was a cold blast of air and the cat, which had been purring contentedly round my ankles, fled, every hair on its body standing on end. It was several hours before my mother plucked up the courage to go back and relock the door, seemingly unlocked, yet I had seen her turning the heavy key which required several twists to secure it. This never happened again.

Many years later, when I was grown up, I took my mother to Switzerland for a holiday. Amidst all the cleanliness – never a discarded chocolate wrapper in the pristine streets, they're as clean as the snow white mountain tops, so it doesn't seem a likely country to be haunted, but I suppose ghosts don't choose geographically. We were visiting a strange town, Basle, I think. And it was spick and span, like everywhere else, and there wasn't much to see except a modern Art Gallery. So we went in, and were quickly bored by the paintings. My mother went back to the street in search of refreshment, but I was drawn to some steps that led down to a cellar. It was very dark and murky, but I could just make out a large chest, covered in worn green leather and embellished with faint painted gold scrolls. Against my better judgement, I felt pulled towards it and at once I was enveloped by a fog of something that felt gooey and sticky but was invisible yet definitely evil. I felt I was being smothered and choked to death. Terrified, I fought it as best I could, and with a desperate breaststroke I forced myself in the direction of the stairs. I reached them eventually, and as I climbed, the clinging mist, or whatever it was, receded.

I was still panting for breath as I rejoined my mother, who was licking an ice-cream cone in the street. "Whatever's the matter?" asked Marje. "You look positively green." What to say? How to explain the unexplainable?

As I grew up I got more worried about these psychic turns. For several years together there would be nothing, and then suddenly – Wham! Bang! – something completely weird or unaccountable would happen. Like the name of a race horse popping into the back of my mind and lodging there. Yes, it did happen, just once, and in the end I put a pound on each way and it did win and yes, I got a modest amount. But, and this is probably why it didn't happen again, part of my mind argued that it might also mean the horse was going to be killed in the race. Oh, beware, beware of psychic omens! They can bode ill, and frequently do, rather than bringing good fortune.

Once, when I was going through a particularly bad patch, I went into the big Lyons Tea house in Piccadilly for a quick coffee. The tables were crowded, and fairly soon a nice lady asked if she could join me. Lost in my own thoughts, I nodded. A little while later we got into conversation, and somehow ESP, which was occupying so much of my thoughts at the time, was mentioned. And my new companion was Rosalind Heywood, an authority and author of many books on the subject. Hesitantly at first, I told her of some of my "happenings" and she immediately calmed my fears. She explained that once upon a time, back in the dark ages, ESP was the way everyone communicated. And everyone still has the power to do so, if they really want to, and could be still and quiet enough in the continual racket of our age. In my case, if I really didn't want this gift, she advised me to look to my health. I realised things had only happened when I was very low, if not properly ill.

I managed to tell Rosalind about my one great certainty: the memory that's been with me as far back as I can remember anything at all, and seems to have been with me since my very beginning. It's a certainty I have about my death in the twelfth century. I "see" the picture as clearly as if it was yesterday. Everything is beige-coloured: beige walls, I'm lying under some sort of beige coverlet. I'm dying in childbirth. The pain is indescribable, overriding everything. I'm longing for death, I can hardly breathe. I know I'm crying, gasping, calling for some sort of relief. Behind me a voice speaks with a quiet authority: "Someone is coming from Canterbury who will make you well –."

After hearing my story Rosalind just nodded and said quietly, "Some of us very old souls carry the burden of other lives with us –." I was relieved to have been believed and understood. But that is why, meeting strangers, I often ask them if they have any connection with Canterbury? Is there someone, somewhere, whom I'm still destined to meet?

I also told Rosalind the lighter story about the time in my School Certificate year, when I received an urgent ESP message from my pony who was in her field about ten minutes away from the house. It was five o'clock in the morning, and a school day (I was working hard for my exams) so I wasn't intending to visit her. But the message came clearly that Gypsy needed help, and without a moment's hesitation I got up and dressed and taking a halter, bicycled up to the field. My thoroughbred Gypsy had come on heat, and in her excitement had attempted to jump the barbed wire fence. Poor Gypsy had a number of nasty cuts and was feeling very sorry for herself. Wheeling my bike, I led her back to the house and made her comfortable in the stable. My mother took over, ordering me to get ready for school and promising to ring the Vet. When I returned at tea time I found all was well. The Vet had been and dressed Gypsy's wounds, remarking that they could have turned nasty if they hadn't been treated promptly. Thanks to her ESP call for help, Gypsy was soon well again and as excitable as ever.

Rosalind also agreed that when you get strong ESP feelings, it's difficult to know how to interpret them. They can be a forewarning of something good or may be warning you off something quite dangerous. Beverley, my friend from the "Dick Whittington" panto, went out to Rome to study classical singing. Soon her mother joined her out there and they invited me out to Rome for a number of wonderful holidays. As a jobbing actress, this was just possible for me – in those days, night flights were very cheap. Beverley supported her singing studies with teaching English and eventually she married a handsome Italian. But alas, less than six months after the wedding, Beverley died of cancer.

Going out to Rome on these night flights was wonderfully exciting. On the drive from the Airport into the city, I would watch the night sky turn green before the full glory of the sunrise. Beverley would set her work aside for the days of my visit, and was quite prepared to drive her little Fiat miles down the coast, so that we could bathe on some secluded beach. And if my visit was in the spring, we would picnic in the Tuscan Hills, among the Etruscan tombs, all overgrown with grass and brambles, in those days seemingly unopened. Now, I suppose it's all been cleaned up and is a Site of National Importance, with the graves opened to a fee-paying public. But we frolicked in the undergrowth and I met my first snake in the long grass. I nearly had a heart attack as I watched it slither away, but it was probably just as frightened as I was. Beverley was deeply jealous of this encounter – despite living in Italy for some years – she'd never seen one like that.

On one holiday, my ESP feelings began as the day of my departure drew near. Normally I have no fear of flying – I relish the miracle of floating above the clouds and getting a bird's eye view of the world below (though I always keep my fingers tightly crossed and offer a quick prayer on landings and take-off.) But this time, my feelings of doom grew and grew, until Beverley, a firm believer in trusting one's intuition, suggested I should change my flight. So I rang the Airline and managed to secure a seat on a different plane, but still on the same day.

I was still worrying as Beverley waved me off at the Airport. I told myself that I'd taken every precaution. I'd changed my flight hadn't I? But my fears escalated when the Captain, in his initial speech, warned of turbulence ahead. We were to keep our seat belts fastened throughout the flight. The first hour wasn't too bad – we rocked about a bit – and I hoped that was the turbulence that'd been mentioned. Then, after another half-hour, we met the storm. It was as if the plane was being tossed about in anger, it seemed too small and fragile to survive such battering. The air hostesses, holding on where they could, were checking the children's safety belts. The plane turned steeply on its side. One of the children started crying. With horrified fascination, I watched the lightning playing along the wing as if it would strike into the very cabin itself. The plane was a Boeing. (In those days there was a saying, "Boeing, Boeing, Gone.") Then with no warning, we nosed into a steep dive. My insides fell into my boots and in that instant all the lockers came open and the hand luggage came crashing down. And there was shouting. Out of the corner of my eye I saw a stewardess grab a baby from the seat parallel with mine. Kneeling in the aisle, she cradled and bent over it. The terrifying descent continued. Now I was in the crouching forward position you're supposed to take in emergencies. The noise had died down, replaced by whispered prayers. My dry lips moved, "Forgive us our trespasses..." Every single soul on that plane was praying. Quarrels, spites, hurts were all forgotten, as in that moment the miracle happened. Somehow, the pilot managed to pull the plane out of the seemingly endless dive. We all felt the terrible physical wrench as he managed to straighten out. I don't think a single word was spoken by anyone for the rest of the flight back to London. My mother met me at Gloucester Road. (Where the Air Terminal was then). "My goodness, you do look green. Was it something you ate on the plane?" How to explain I'd failed miserably to interpret helpful ESP warnings correctly?

The time came for me to have a cataract removed. This op. had been looming for ages, and I'd managed to save enough Insurance from the Covent Garden accident to have it done privately, as this op. is so much a "sausage factory" when done on the NHS. Or so I was told. I'd already had some trouble with my left eye, and some years before I'd been recommended to a wonderful man at the London Clinic. He'd told me that I had a burn behind the eye – I must have looked at the sun as a child. He warned me that I might have trouble with the retina wrinkling as I grew older. I had such faith in this eye surgeon I asked PPP if he could do my cataract op., but they said "No." Apparently I had to have someone from the Edward VII. What's good enough for Royalty, I thought, and went ahead. Later, I learnt that PPP own the Edward VII Hospital, and they make you go there (though, incidentally, the London Clinic is cheaper) so that in effect you're paying them back with their own money, all that you've already paid them in your PPP Insurance premiums, plus the cost of their surgeon and the op.

I knew none of the names of the doctors I was offered there, and had no idea how to choose an eye surgeon. But a woman I knew slightly from my computer class had had her cataracts done by a man from the Edward VII, and she spoke highly of him. "This lady," I argued with myself, "worked at Bletchley during the War. She knows a thing or two." So I notified PPP, and duly went to see this surgeon for a pre-op examination at his Harley Street consulting rooms. It was coming up to Christmas, and I daresay the man was rushed. It certainly seemed so. The examination was anything but thorough, and he didn't seem to be listening when I described my visits to Mr. L. at the London Clinic. Mr. L.'s concern about the burn and my retina was brushed aside, and nothing was noted down about it. In my infinite ignorance, I presumed this man had at least seen the burn when he examined the back of my eye.

But over and above everything else was

my intuition, which was screaming from every pore of my body, "Get away from this man, leave NOW!" But alack and alas, once more I didn't heed what I was being so plainly told. I put all my feelings down to my terror about the coming operation. I was stone cold-petrified – the idea of lying down on a slab with only a local anaesthetic, and someone slicing into your eye, "oh, the horror!" (As Conrad said, about something quite different.) It was the horror of the op. itself, not this man, that was sending the warning signals teeming through my brain, o, so once more I argued with myself. A date for the op. had been fixed in January, best get it over and done with, I thought. If I changed anything now, it would only prolong the agony. It'll soon be over, and I can forget all about it.

There was no faulting the Edward VII Hospital itself. I had a lovely room, and my own nurse. She was a comforting New Zealander, and she kept reassuring me that I would feel absolutely nothing during the op. (I didn't.) And lovely John Newbury spent the whole day sitting in my room with me, and laughing at things – as he always did. (Oh, God, how I miss him. He had a stroke one Christmas Day – when we were doing "Bohème" – John had always been a waiter. He did make a partial recovery, but his friend Toby spirited him away to a new life in Maidenhead and wouldn't allow me to continue having any contact with John. Not for the first time. It broke my heart.) When I was discharged, John duly took me home in a taxi, and there was a lot more laughing – about Mimi, or was it Perdy then? – being a guide cat. My left eye was completely bandaged over.

I went to my surgeon's Harley Street rooms the next morning. He whipped the bandages off, and said, expectantly, "Well?" I held my hand over my right eye. It took me some time to mouth the words, "I … can't…see." I was struggling. There was something that might have been a door – but it was far off. There was the first faint sounds of unease in the Dr.'s voice.

"Oh well. It often takes a few days to settle. Come and see me on Friday." By Friday, with my left eye I could see shapes – dimly. But where were the clear bright colours everyone who had had cataract operations told me to expect? Eventually, I learnt that I'd lost 60% of sight in that eye. It seemed, as the man at the London Clinic had foretold, my retina had wrinkled with age. Too late, I understood that if you have a wrinkled retina, it must be straightened out before a cataract operation is performed. My surgeon claimed he hadn't seen the burn when he examined my eyes on that pre-op visit. Which seemed strange, when an optician in Boots had actually spotted it – it was this man who'd originally sent me to Mr. L. at the London Clinic, all that time ago.

Then the fireworks began. The eye specialist, obviously terrified that I would sue him (as if I would, after all the trauma of the Covent Garden affair?) sent me the most abusive letter I've ever received. He blamed me, my GP, and even the Boots' optician. He told me he'd performed 10,000 cataract ops, and had had only five failures. As I was one of the latter, it was hardly helpful. He swore blind – no that isn't the right phrase for these circumstances – that he'd looked at the back of my eye and seen neither the burn nor my wrinkled retina. He was obviously not going to admit any blame, but I did feel he owed me something after such gross negligence, and I tried to get him to pay for me to see the Head of Retinas at Moorfields, who, I'd been told, was the person who might be able to restore some of the sight to my left eye. But he refused. I made the same request to PPP, who, after all, had forced me to go to the Edward VII. They also turned down my request.

In my distress, I turned to Mr. L. at the London Clinic. As I had no more private insurance, he very kindly wrote to the Retina Head Man at Moorfields, and asked him to see me as a personal favour. Which he did. Some time later, I met the wonderful Hungarian, who eventually persuaded me to have the extremely tricky (and painful) operation (on the NHS) that did restore some sight to that eye. I was interested that Mr. L. said that if the surgeon who did the damage had only asked him, he would have shown him the original notes about the burn at the back of my eye.

Eventually, some sight was restored to that eye, but it has remained partially damaged. Two or three years later, I had the cataract on the other eye successfully removed at Moorfields on the NHS, with no unfortunate repercussions.

But why, oh why, didn't I listen to my

intuition, which told me to run away forever from that Harley Street consulting room that snowy December afternoon? Would I never learn to trust my own feelings?

And then there was Knossos. Since I was quite young I knew I had to go there. But sufficient funds for a holiday in Crete didn't come my way until I was quite old. After all the bills were paid (the Cat Carer's one was quite the largest, and I only had Mimi with me for some of the three years) I used what was left of the Covent Garden compensation money for a few wonderful little holidays. And every bit of Crete was magic – from meeting Celia, to all the expeditions and guides.

First we went to the 19ᵗʰ Century Monastery of Kardiotissa. As we left, a nun pressed a hunk of Holy Bread into my hand. It was too hard for me, but the little donkey I was to ride up the mountain enjoyed it. Our next visit was to the Dikteon Cave. After my ride, I dismounted near to the entrance to Zeus' Cave. I left the elderly donkey-man and his charge to enjoy a well-earned rest, and I began my descent into the darkness. I went slowly – the steps were slippery. Sometimes the beam from a friendly Guide's torch illuminated the grotesque stalagmites and stalactites – here was one resembling the face of Kronos, who according to legend, devoured five of Zeus' siblings. Another was said to represent Rhea, his mother, holding the precious infant, here in the cave where she'd hidden him from his vengeful father and saved his life. There was a trickle of water into a subterranean pool, and the atmosphere was heavy with the memories of all the different cults and ceremonies held there down the centuries.

The climb back up was hard. But outside, in the bright sunshine, Skinos, my little donkey, and her owner were waiting. I remounted Skinos, and we set off down the perilous path. The donkey-man hummed as he led his charge. I clung to the pommel. On my left, the mountainside fell away precipitately. To my right, the closely-packed olive trees whispered among themselves. My little donkey picked her way among the stones and boulders as delicately as a dancer. It was midday, and the air was very still. The path was deserted. Quite alone, it seemed we three became part of Crete, part of all her myths and legends and stories. The donkey-man sang some long forgotten air, and we made our way slowly down the mountain.

And the next day we were to go to Knossos. I'd discussed some of the stories with Carlos, a hardened Cretan guide. He insisted that the myths and legends had grown out of things that had really happened – fires and earthquakes and invading Barbarian tribes.

Then, the night before our visit to Knossos, I had a dream. It was as real as if I'd stepped outside myself, asleep in the hotel bedroom, and was standing on the quay at Piraeus. My Greek mother knelt beside me. She was weeping and wringing her hands. I was in a group of other youths and maidens. We wore simple white tunics.

My mother's worn fingers kept creeping up to touch the bonds that tied my wrists. Our heads had been shaved – that had been the worst part – the humiliation greater than the fear. Or the resulting itch. My other self, asleep in the hotel, paused there. It came to me that the historians didn't know about the head shaving – I'd never read it anywhere. But then we were being roughly pushed towards the waiting ship, and the thought vanished. If we proved good enough, the ring awaited us. At least the bull was quick. Otherwise, and I already knew it was the scullions for me, and the fate was worse.

So I went to Knossos. And for the day became just one of the hordes of tourists stumbling over the uneven stones, complaining about the heat, marvelling at the bright frescoes, and taking photos of everything.

Our party was led by a wonderful guide, Maria. She believed all the myths about Knossos, though with Carlos she insisted they grew out of real happenings. When I asked her about the Minotaur, she looked quizzical, but assured me there were still miles of as yet unexcavated passages beneath the Palace. "Who knows what they may one day reveal?" and she smiled knowingly.

It's said everyone who visits thinks they've been to Knossos before. As our party wheeled left, I felt a quite desperate urge to turn away. For a brief second, beyond the ruins, dazzled by the bright sunlight, I saw the highly-coloured Palace as it once was: busy and populated. But there was no escaping the tourist trail. I turned to follow my party.

But in that instant, I asked for a sign. The stones of Knossos are swept clean. No speck of ash or shred of paper is allowed to defile them. I looked down. At my feet was an eagle's feather – light brown, darker, deepening towards the quill. I had been given my answer.

And tonight, as I lie trapped in my bed, my right leg immobilised in its iron cage, waiting for the night to pass, I'm looking at that feather. It's on my bookcase now.

There was another holiday I remember when I was much older. It was a package tour of Turkey and we were taken to some of the First World War cemeteries on the Gallipoli peninsula. After the excitement of crossing the Dardanelles, it was a sobering journey. I went first to one perched on the cliff's edge. Beyond the serried rows of white slabs, some forever blank, there was the sheer drop to the sea. That day it was calm and azure, but still the memories of the thousands of ANZAC soldiers slaughtered there during the ill-fated attacks of 1915 were too hard to bear.

I turned inland, and opened the gate of Lone Pine Cemetery. It was deserted, and then, seemingly from nowhere, a golden retriever suddenly appeared. His flagged tail was wagging in welcome, clearly he was saying, "I'm so glad you've come to visit my boys." Having greeted me, he immediately began to lead the way down the field between the rows of graves. He seemed to know exactly where he was going; once or twice he looked back over his shoulder. I gathered I was meant to follow, so I did. Suddenly he stopped and sat down on the cropped grass. He had positioned himself carefully between two of the identical white stones. I examined the inscriptions. One was a captain, aged 24, the other a private, a boy of 18. They'd both given their lives on the same day in 1915. I looked at the dog. His tail was thumping the ground rhythmically. He stared. Something was expected of me. And so I prayed. In my heart, and in a beseeching whisper, for these two heroes who had given their lives so long ago, and now lay here in their last unadorned resting place.

At last the dog seemed satisfied. Without a final look, he wandered off in the direction of the giant conifer that gives its name to the cemetery. I made my way slowly back to the gate. Tears were streaming down my face. At the entrance, one of our party, an Indian lady, had come to look for me. She put a comforting arm round my shoulders. "Enough cemeteries for today. Time for a coffee." She led me away.

I got no psychic warnings about the sudden death of my Father. Just a bleak telephone call on November 11th 1963. I'd barely seen him since I was nine years old. And now he'd gone, leaving me with a nothingness and submerged dreams. My informant was Mr. Blankansee, Punch's solicitor, who was to befriend me for the next two years. He told me that Punch had died leaving many debts. Peter and I, as "The only children of the full blood," had inherited these. (!!??) For some reason, I can't remember why, we weren't allowed to go bankrupt, which would have been so much easier. Mr. Blankansee, smartly dressed in his velvet-collared overcoat, accompanied me when I went to inspect my Father's flat in Victoria. I was somewhat shocked to find it so threadbare. Much later I realised the first mistress had stripped it of anything of value. She even had the nerve to explain to me that my Father – a Lieutenant-Colonel, "Didn't own a watch"!! Punch had been undergoing a big operation in the Military Hospital, and, against all advice, had discharged himself for the Service of Remembrance at the Albert Hall on the Saturday evening. The Lady claimed to have found him dead on the Monday morning... She also managed to get Peter on her side by taking him out to a meal after the Remembrance service. I searched the flat, but there was no sign of Punch's mediocre medals. I never knew if Peter or the first mistress nabbed them. I knew my Father had been awarded the Victorian Order (fourth class) for writing the official History of the Royal Tournament; and also a history of Kneller Hall.

I saw Punch's red-haired second wife twice, but I never spoke to her. I believe she had a son from her previous marriage, about the same age as Peter. Her marriage to Punch had long broken up, but I don't know when that happened. She came to his funeral and the Memorial Service in the Guard's Chapel. On both occasions she earned my respect by sitting discreetly near the back, as Marje and I did. At the Memorial the front row was occupied by three sobbing mistresses. Peter joined them, though he didn't cry. My mother sat stoically through the service, but towards the end I could tell she was breaking up. I whisked her away, and we waited on the corner of Buckingham Palace Road while I tried, desperately and unsuccessfully, to get a taxi. In those horrendous few minutes I formulated the idea of learning to drive. So I did.

The fact that Peter was siding with the First Mistress – but then he hadn't seen our Father's ransacked flat – put me in an even more difficult position. For the following two years Mr. Blankansee, the solicitor, sent me documents that required both our signatures. I dealt with mine promptly and then forwarded them to my brother, who invariably took two or three weeks to send them back. It all took endless time, but the solicitor was cleverly placing the few valuables of Punch's that remained – these included a drum that had been made into a coffee table, (I suppose the First Mistress wasn't able to roll it away in the middle of the night) in specialist sales. In the end he made enough to completely clear all of Punch's debts. But it meant that for more than two years I couldn't take any acting work. I kept body and soul together working at Exhibitions and coffee bars. I only resumed my theatrical life when my Father's name was completely cleared. So the man who'd never given me anything at all, except the precious gift of life itself – greedily snatched away more than two years of my life. I did feel a bit resentful.

CHAPTER FOURTEEN

The magic of radio – or why it's better being a waxwork

1958 – 1974

I always thought the wireless was magic and I longed to be on it and cast these spells myself. My first chance to broadcast came when I was at Lichfield, ostensibly "resting." In fact I was nursing my Grandfather through the weeks of dementia that preceded his death. (Before his body was cold, one of the Cathedral Canons burst into the house and told me and Marje that we'd got to move out by the end of the month. My Grandfather had lived in that house for twenty-nine years. So much for the Christian Charity in the Close.)

But back to radio. During those unhappy weeks I chanced to hear a Children's Hour programme from the North. They were inviting teenagers to write in if they'd had an unusual job. I answered, hoping that playing Dick Whittington's Cat would fit this description. Apparently it did and I was invited up to Manchester and made my first broadcast from my own script. I think I was paid two guineas.

A year or two later, I came to London and did the usual round of BBC radio auditions. My voice still sounded very young and I began getting the odd part playing children and teenagers. These included one in "The Go-Between" – with a Norfolk accent which came in handy later when I did "Roots" at Windsor. I was in an interesting documentary about Charlotte Street. I played Nina Hamnett, and a member of the cast who'd known her actually said, "You don't look a bit like her!" How to point out we were "on air" not telly? I did some fascinating schools' broadcasts, which included being the voice of a violet; and once being told off because I "wasn't thinking from the 'Golly' point of view."

But the most exciting production I did was for Christopher Sykes, then the doyen of producers at Broadcasting House. He expressed a wish to meet me. I was ushered into his presence. It was like going to meet God. He was a very large man and his head was huge. All I remember is that he waved a waggish finger at me and said, "We have plans for you, young lady." Sometime later I heard that I was to play The Maidservant in his prestigious production of Ivy Compton Burnett's "Manservant and Maidservant." The Scullery Boy was played by the lovely Melvyn Hayes who later came to well-deserved fame in "It Ain't Half Hot Mum." We had an unprecedented entire week for rehearsals, and I got much help and support from the legendary broadcaster Marjorie Westbury, who played the Cook. At 4'10" she was a bustling power of energy, and quite unique in her mastery of microphone technique. The production enjoyed some success, before fading quietly into the annals of Broadcasting.

I was more than a little surprised when I was asked to join the cast of "Mrs. Dale's Diary," a daily radio soap that chronicled the goings-on in a suburban family. At its height it was enormously popular and ran, in all, for nearly a decade. At first mine was a temporary posting. I was supposed to be Mrs. Dale's fourteen year old niece, popping into the family life on a short visit from Canada.

I was accompanied by my twelve year old brother, ably played by Glyn Dearman. Much later he became a radio producer in his own right and despite the hours we spent together in the corner of studios practising our Canadian accents, he never once offered me a job! Strangely, it seemed we were a success with the listeners. After our initial stint, we were retired for a few weeks, and then reappeared in the scripts, both having aged by four years. (This gave the writers more scope – suddenly I was old enough to be employed as a nurse.)

Much was written about the Dales, and certainly in my time, most of it was true. Ellis Powell was then Mrs. Dale and she was a very strange lady, probably closer to the mythical Sister George, said to be modelled on her, than might be imagined. The rest of the cast seethed with petty intrigues and jealousies, even my innocent talks with James Dale, who played Dr. Dale, were suspect. My recording sessions were made a misery by the Australian actress who played my mother. She made a determined attempt to take over the running of my life. But she did get her well known agent to take me onto her books, though my time with Josephine Burton was quickly curtailed by her untimely death. Josephine was also Joan Plowright's agent. Joan, at the time, was secretly engaged to Olivier. They were both in New York for Joan's opening in "Roots." Josephine went out for the first night and her appendix burst. She had no medical insurance and she was dead before Olivier could be tapped for the necessary funds that would have saved her life.

I had the luck, though it did not help my popularity, to be the only family member not to be under sole contract to the BBC. This meant that I could do other acting jobs as well. I remember I did two tours during my Dale years. The main producer, Betty Davies, was very good about recording my scenes in the lunch hour or evenings, when I was employed elsewhere. And of course the money was wonderful. There was a certain repeat of the programme every morning. (The main episode went out at 4.15pm.) I managed to save much of my repeat money, and bought my first Mini with it. But all in all, I was not too sorry when Janet was finally written out of the script.

Almost immediately I started broadcasting for the BBC on the Overseas Service at Bush House. (A worldly cousin of my mother kindly called it my War Service. Sometimes it felt like it.) At this time I was more or less a unit with the playwright David Campton. He'd written a thrilling radio serial "The

Missing Jewel" which was bought by what we called "Araby." All the different Arab states had saved up their meagre drama allowance and were squandering it all on one big production. Of course I had to audition for the principal girl's part, and was on tenterhooks for several weeks until I heard I was to play her. It was the most ingenious production and we all had a wonderful time rehearsing and recording it. The director had hugely ambitious plans to promote the production with publicity, including some exciting photo calls. Alas, I only just managed to stagger through the final recording session, being doubled up with internal pains. As soon as the wrap was called I was rushed to hospital for an emergency op.

I was out of action for some weeks but once recovered I found there was more work waiting for me at Bush House. I spent many long hours doing the Overseas Teaching programmes, endlessly repeating things like "The cat sat on the mat" with different inflexions. Some of the work was more exciting – these were the days of the 33⅓ vinyl records. David wrote "The Gates of Troy" which had a very starry cast – I declaimed my way through Cassandra's prophecies. One of the old directors there even asked me to play Cathy in a 15 minute adaptation of "Wuthering Heights." As one of nature's Isabellas, this was a grave mistake and may have marked my departure from Bush House, after exactly 4½ years, once again.

But the works of the Brontë sisters seem to have been woven into my acting life. I played

Isabella Lynton, with great success, and cozzies from the dressing-up box at Lichfield, during my Rep. season at Newcastle-under-Lyme. BBC TV's religious department sent me to Derby Cathedral to read a selection of Charlotte Brontë's letters. Their cameras were there for a "Songs of Praise," and as the Beeb were too mean to provide a costume, I wore a dress I bought especially at a posh shop in Sloane Street.

Long before I was properly into TV I squeezed in as a Lowood Schoolgirl in the best-ever "Jane Eyre." Daphne Slater was peerless in this title rôle. I frisked around as a French school girl when BBC TV did "Villette" as their classic serial. I had to harass Jill Bennett (in French) who was playing the lead, Lucy Snow, until she finally lost patience with me and twisted my neck and pushed me into a cupboard. Jill was so nice she hated doing this and I had a lot of difficulty getting her to do it so that it looked realistic.

Julia Trevelyan Oman was the great designer who did the sets and costumes for "Bohème." We all got to know her even better when she did "Die Fledermaus" at Covent Garden. (She designed our dresses individually.) Later she was asked by Madame Tussaud's to design a set of waxworks based on the Brontë family and Branwell's famous painting of his sisters. Julia asked me to sit for Charlotte and Pauline was to be Emily. Branwell actually painted himself out of the portrait but Madame Tussaud's wanted him in so Mark (the Cook in Bohème) came too. One summer evening we all went to the huge building in Baker Street. We were taken in the lift up to the workshops on the top floor. I shall never forget the looks on the faces of the technicians who were going to model the waxworks. We were all much, much too fat. (And I, still smoking twenty Senior Service a day, was at my thinnest.) The Brontës were so tiny they were almost munchkins. But the workers at Madame Tussaud's were stuck with us. So, smiling gamely, they took hundreds of photographs and measurement from us, and were preparing to shave off many inches for the actual waxworks. They were kind enough to invite us to the opening party and it was a fascinating evening. After viewing the Brontë family immortalised, I had a good wander round. I was particularly struck by the Sleeping Beauty dutifully awaiting her Prince to awaken her. Her chest heaved up and down in a totally unrealistic manner. I was so glad the Brontë's hadn't been made to breathe.

Lovely Peter Wildeblood (goodness he was attractive!) asked me to be in one or two of the Gilbert and Sullivan comic operas he was doing for radio. In the end I was in nearly all of them as luckily my speaking voice matched the soprano who was singing all the youngest parts: the Littlest Fairy, the teenager at the Academy for Young Ladies, etc. Patricia Routledge was the only person talented enough to do both the singing and the speaking of her rôles. In one of the recordings, I was partnered with her to do some ad-libbing, something I've always adored. I was extremely proud when she exclaimed, "Goodness, I didn't know you were a funny lady!" At the first rehearsal, Peter told us all we were going to make our fortunes: the BBC recordings would be unique, no one had ever made Gilbert and Sullivan records in their entirety with all the spoken dialogue included. The Beeb promised they were going to market them and sell them worldwide.

Only of course they didn't. Instead I received letter after letter from the BBC saying I'd been overpaid and they wanted some money back. Living on a shoestring as I did, I was terribly upset and determined not to repay them. An actor called Derek Birch took up my case with Equity. But the crafty Beeb got their money alright. In those days (oh happy times) I worked for them a lot, and they simply deducted some money from every cheque they sent, until the so-called debt was paid. The wonderful comic writers Norden and Muir were caught in the same way and they simply wrote back, "We have no apparatus for the returning of funds," and got away with it. Or so they said.

Two of the loveliest vocal jobs I ever did were Son-et-Lumières, that curious hybrid of radio and a lighting show. Through some friends I was asked to play Mary, Queen of Scots, in the Son-et-Lumière for St. Andrews. I lapped up Antonia Fraser's biography, and decided to play her with a French accent. (After all, she was brought up at the French Court, and we're always told we retain the voices from our youth.) John Knox was to be played by Andrew Faulds, an MP and at that time Father of the

House. He said he was too busy to come to rehearsals so I went to Westminster and somewhat ironically we rehearsed their vocally sparring scenes on the terrace of the House of Commons. Robert Harris was to be the narrator.

I never saw the finished production in situ, but there was a showing or playing of the sound recording. Robert Harris was there with his partner, a famous radio producer. They both came up to me afterwards and said, simultaneously, "Your scenes made us cry!" Of course I was pleased by this compliment but in the years that followed the famous radio producer never offered me any work, although they'd obviously both been moved by my performance.

Christopher Ede had been promising me a job for a long time. He'd rung to say he thought I could play Consuelo Vanderbilt, the 9th Duchess, in a story of the Churchill family for the Blenheim Son-et-Lumière, if I could do a Boston accent. (I eventually found a student at LAMDA to coach me for this.) The great excitement was that Richard Burton was going to play the Dukes and Sir Winston Churchill. Consuelo was one of the many wives. And I missed the chance of acting with the legendary Burton, because I was in a play for schools at the Mermaid. Christopher very kindly recorded my part in a different sound booth on a different day. But I was so sad at missing out on my only chance to be Mrs. Richard Burton. Apparently they had a wonderful day in the studio for the real recording. Drinks for everyone flowed and by the end of the day the studio was knee deep in empties. To make up for my disappointment, I drove Marje out to Blenheim to see a performance of the Son-et-Lumière. As it grew dark, the music dimmed and one by one the lights began to come on in the great house. And then Richard's majestic voice began telling the moving story of the Churchill family. Gradually the other voices chimed in – it was all very exciting. There was fog on the road but I drove back to London in record time, with the growling tones of Richard's Churchill still ringing in my ears.

CHAPTER FIFTEEN

Acting with animals

1962 – 2002

"Animals are such agreeable friends – they ask no questions, they pass no criticisms." George Eliot

In the long three years of my isolated incarceration, I never lost hope of regaining my life as a jobbing actress. But in that first terrible year there was another blow. A fat brown envelope arrived in the post. I opened it and out spilled hundreds of photos and all the contracts I'd had with my agent, Simon. There was a nice letter from him, too. He said he hated having to do this when I was having such a bad time, but, regretfully, he'd decided to give up being a theatrical agent. He said his heart wasn't in it any more, and he'd lost his enthusiasm. And he was very, very sorry. (He went on to work most successfully with ACAS.)

And that, of course, made my prospects even bleaker. Then, when all seemed over as regards my ever working again, I received a tentative offer of a job that it seemed I just might be able to do – as the part was a woman in a wheelchair!

Hope revived, I looked after myself and worked even harder on my exercises. When I next went to the clinic at Kings (nowadays I wore the boxer shorts provided by Pauline) and saw Mr. Groom, I told him about the little film. The lovely man was absolutely delighted for me and agreed that if I continued to make good progress, this was a job I should be able to do. Alas, when the time came to give a final answer to the film people, my leg had been re-broken, I was wearing the Ilizarov frame to lengthen it, and was thoroughly sick and heavily bed-bound. Oh, the disappointment.

The offer had come about because I'd made another highly successful short film for these people, "The Tea Party" – scenes from it were on my showreel for the year. In it I had a little dog – a jolly Jack Russell terrier who loved his job and was perfectly trained. He was, like me, a professional. In practically every scene he had to follow me about closely, at my heel. His trainer, an old hand, showed me what to do to make this happen. Johnny and I were introduced. I gave him a little bit of sausage meat that made me a friend for life. Once my hands had been smeared with a bit more, Johnny was ready to follow me anywhere on the set. Everyone in the cast of "The Tea Party" was lovely, and we seemed to laugh non-stop. After the other one, when I wasn't the lady-in-the-wheelchair, I was told how much I'd been missed.

I looked back at the other adventures I'd had acting with livestock. My very first television was for Kevin Sheldon – I'd got it by writing to him. (Things were very different in those days – your letters were sometimes answered.) Back then, BBC TV had a religious slot for children at 5pm on Sundays. I was to be in a dramatisation of the story of Moses and I was playing his youngest daughter. The drama was Moses' staff turning into a serpent. This was played by a real boa constrictor and was an unfortunate beginning to my TV career, since I not only fear snakes but am allergic to a point of feeling quite ill when I'm anywhere near one. (My brother once told me I was taken to the London Zoo when I was about four. He said entering the Reptile House I screamed and fell into a fit and it took the rest of the day to calm my fears – I have no recollection at all of this event.)

I must say the snake we had in "Moses" was very professional. It came to rehearsals in a large zip tartan bag. Ever since I have kept well away from large zipped bags placed on the floor of the Underground. And it's not because I think they might contain a bomb! Anyway, I avoided it as much as possible at rehearsals, but when we came to transmission there was no escape. The performance was, of course, transmitted live, like all TV in those days. As Moses' youngest daughter, I was right at the front of the family group. Since there could be no pausing, with cunning sleight of hand from stage hands, the staff was passed off one way, and the boa constrictor handed on, directly in front of me. Oh, Mamma Mia! I think what saved me was the lovely old actor playing Moses. He'd fathomed my upset, and as we came to do the scene he whispered, "Don't worry if you faint – I'll catch you. I'm right behind you." But I wasn't there, I was far away being Moses' youngest daughter so I got through that and the live repeated performance on the following Thursday.

Incidentally, one of my out-of-work jobs was on W.H. Smith's stand at the Schoolboys' Exhibition at Olympia. (I won some sort of prize for selling the most fountain pens.) But, so help me, on the next stand was George Cansdale with several large live snakes, which the schoolboys were apt to drape round their necks and wander about with. I just had to set my mind firmly on other things. But George Cansdale sensed my fear and throughout the week kept urging me to touch one. The warmth I would feel, he assured me, would banish my horror forever. But no, no, no, I'm not that brave. Despite his constant pleading, it just couldn't be done.

Birds are a different story – I love them, and during those years I lay trapped on my bed I would watch for them and long to fly. There were two pigeons, of course, in my second TV job, since it was the story of the Willow pattern – "Two Pigeons Flying High." I got this from writing a letter, too. In those days there were very few ethnic professional Chinese actors working in the UK. I somehow heard, or read, about this and wrote to the director, Christian Simpson and sent him a photo of myself playing the little Chinese Princess in "The Princess and the Swineherd" at the Birmingham Rep. I got the part of the Chinese maid servant who helps the lovers to escape. The leading girl was played by a genuine Chinese actress, but her lover was Robert Rietti, who was Italian!

It was written by the poet James Kirkup, so the script was beautiful. I really only just glimpsed the two (professional) pigeons who were released to fly across the screen at the end, as the lovers find their freedom, but they were as beautiful and appeared as free as the ones I saw half a century later in the ballet "The Two Pigeons" at Covent Garden.

I saw much more of the pigeons that were engaged for the production of Maurice Maeterlinck's famous play "The Blue Bird," that I was in at the old Lyric Theatre, Hammersmith. At the end of each performance, one of these birds, as the actual Blue Bird of the title, was released from the stage by the little boy, Tytyl. As he opened the cage he said, "If any of you find the Blue Bird, could you give him back to us? We need him for our happiness, later on." I'd auditioned for the production, and got the part of Water. I played opposite the then well-known dancer, Tommy Merrifield, as Fire. He's now a famous sculptor, who specialises in doing the most wonderful figures of dancers. Twice a year he opens his house and garden on two successive Sundays and every summer I go up to Hampstead and he gives me a warm reception. As the years pass, his stories of our exploits in that production lengthen. It was a wonderful cast, led by Dilys Laye as the Cat, and George Moon played the Dog, and my dear friend David Campton was Bread. John

Hart-Dyke was a consoling member of the cast as The Father and Pamela Lane, who played The Mother, regaled us all with stories of the time she was married to John Osborne.

Although only one pigeon was needed for the production, three had been purchased (probably it was a three for two offer – the management was sorely in need of funds.) Each night one of the three birds was selected to be the star of the evening's performance. How they must have hated their make-up procedure – the chosen bird was unceremoniously dunked in a bucket of Reckitt's Blue by the Assistant Stage Manager. Once it had dried off, and this couldn't be done with a towel for fear of losing the precious colour, it was put in the wicker cage, ready for Tytyl to carry on and release it at the end of the play.

The "blue" bird then circled the auditorium and hopefully returned to join us, the cast, as we lined up for the curtain call. But no one had realised that although two of the birds were trained homing pigeons, the third was not. It may have been a wild one, illegally snatched from Trafalgar Square. In due time, this one got its big chance. Tytyl (James Hunter) said his immortal line, and delighted with its sudden freedom, the rogue bird soared into the auditorium, made several swoops round, dropped its doings on the dress circle and finally found a nesting perch high in the eaves of the Lyric Theatre. After a bit of a wait, the curtain came down and we all went home. I heard later that the stage management spent the entire night with nets on long poles trying to entice the reluctant bird to return to what was, of course, the end of its brief stage career. I expect it made Sunday lunch for the management.

"The Blue Bird" hadn't been presented in London for many years, and the Box Office was an immediate sell-out. But on Christmas Eve the snow began to fall. We'd done a dress rehearsal cum charity matinée in aid of the RSPCA and the rather amateurish girl playing Light (rumour had it, she'd paid to be in the production) was bitten by a kangaroo in the foyer. The snow continued through Christmas Day, while we were all at home stuffing ourselves (or celebrating the Religious Festival, each to his own) and preparing for the Boxing Day opening. While we struggled to Hammersmith through the ever growing snowdrifts, the phone in the Box Office never stopped ringing with cancelled bookings.

So we ploughed on, facing increasingly meagre audiences. It grew more and more difficult to get to the theatre, but I was lucky as I lived quite near. David Campton came to stay with us, leaving his temporary lodgings in Swiss Cottage. Then we sheltered Pauline Williams, who was playing the principal part of 'Night' so elegantly, when it became impossible for her to get back to her home in Surrey. After every show the posh little girl who played Mytyl was whisked home to Knightsbridge by her Daddy, in his large car. As we stamped our feet at the snowy bus stop we gazed enviously at the empty seats in his limousine.

The last night of the Maeterlinck play came and the management, unable to pay our salaries, escaped over the rooftops of Hammersmith taking our Insurance Cards with them. (In those days, these were far more valuable than the money we weren't paid.) Later, Equity, having not collected the last week's salaries for us, paid us in full. We all clubbed together and almost the whole cast scrambled into one taxi, taking us away from "The Blue Bird" forever. Pamela Lane gloated over us – somehow she'd managed to hang onto her Insurance Card, despite the odds.

I had a rather livelier encounter with a parrot when I went up to Newcastle-upon-Tyne to do a few parts at the Playhouse. At that time, it was being run as a repertory theatre by Julian Harrington – who was mad about having live animals (and birds) on stage. He initially engaged me to play one of the young people in "The Ghost Train" – the old original rep stand-by that had been written by Arnold Ridley (known to the world as Private Godfrey in Dad's Army.) There were no theatrical digs to be had – I stayed in a dreadfully pretentious B&B. It may even have been the one that used to advertise "Prunella Scales Loved Staying With Us." In your dreams.

The first few days of rehearsal passed like any other Rep. production. The lead was being played by a rather flashy actress who'd come up from London, like me. Then, as we all began getting the lines under our belts, it became clear that this actress was unable to learn anything. It transpired she'd recently recovered from a dreadful car accident. Rehearsals were halted and Julian Harrington interviewed the cast one by one in his office and explained. When it was my turn and I'd been told the situation, Julian said he was having to juggle the whole cast round and would I mind playing the old character lady Miss Bourne? I jumped at the chance, as I knew character work would be my final destination in the business, but in those days (1963) this seemed very far off. I also knew Miss Bourne slept through Act II. A bonus when it came to learning the lines.

So we all got down to studying our new rôles and Julian, a gentleman-of-the-theatre to his fingertips, kept the lady with the learning difficulties on and paid her salary for the run of "The Ghost Train." She hung around the theatre, and of course we were all very sympathetic, until she started popping into our dressing rooms and giving us notes and telling us all how we should play our parts. Our sympathy quickly evaporated.

One of Sybil Thorndike's granddaughters was also working in the theatre. Formerly an ASM, with this big change-around she was promoted to one of the juvenile rôles. She was also very fully occupied having her first ever affair with Freddie Jones, who'd come up to star in "Figure of Fun," which I was also in. I adored doing this and acting with Freddie, except for one matinée, when he dried, and went down to the audience and explained he'd lost his lines and said winningly, "I'll just do that bit again." In those days, things like that just weren't done. I was standing stage centre, and was dumbfounded. But Freddie, with his innate charm, got away with it. "Figure of Fun" died a death with audiences. It seems they sometimes feel cheated by plays about the theatre. But a few years earlier "On Monday Night" had been a great success. (I used to love playing Daphne.) More recently, Michael Frayn's hilarious "Noises Off" has run and run, and is constantly revived.

Back at the Playhouse, as Dame Sybil's granddaughter made sure we were all kept informed of every scintillating detail of her affair, I got ready to play Miss Bourne. Julian, trying to help me, ordered a special wig from London. It proved too horrendous and I realised it was far simpler and more effective just to put my own hair in a bun. "The Ghost Train" takes place entirely in a station waiting room. In the French's acting edition, it says Miss Bourne has a parrot in a cage among her luggage. Knowing nothing of Julian's passion for live things, I presumed it would be a stuffed one. But at the Monday afternoon dress rehearsal a live parrot, that Julian has found in a local pub, arrived.

All went well for the first two performances with the parrot perching peacefully in its cage on the floor, where I'd carefully placed it, while I feigned sleep. But on the third night, the bird suddenly came to and realised it was missing its chance of stardom. It started squawking at the top of its voice, screeching unmentionable words which it must have picked up in the pub. Rigid with horror, but still pretending to be asleep, I listened as the actors topped up their voices and tried to drown the strident screams issuing from the cage. The dialogue faltered and finally stopped altogether. I knew every eye in the theatre was on me and what I had to do. As nonchalantly as I could, I mimed "surprised waking up." I rose from the bench and picked up the cage and carried the still screeching bird to the set door that was supposed to be locked. The agitated stage manager was waiting for me and as I handed over the ungovernable bird, we received the biggest round of applause I've ever had. Then I tottered back to the bench and resumed my sleeping position and the play continued. So much for acting with animals. And birds.

CHAPTER SIXTEEN

Cheese or chocolate

1962 – 2002

Commercials only came into our lives when ITV started in 1955. Up till then, there had only been the two BBC Channels – strictly no advertising, the policy supposed to be holding good, even today, which is a laugh when the BBC quite shamelessly advertises all its productions and products, ad nauseam.

But pretty soon I was scuttling about London auditioning for these, supposedly, well paid jobs. J. Walter Thompson, in Berkeley Square, was a great source of employment, I remember once presenting myself at the reception desk there, to be asked briskly, "Cheese or Chocolate?" (They were the two products for auditions that day.)

It was from there that I actually got one of my first commercials. I'd been sent by a rather dubious agent, and been told they wanted any number of people in historical costumes. So I chattered on about how period my face was, and how good I looked in old-fashioned cozzies, etc. I actually got the job and really thought I was going to appear as some sort of serving wench. Much to my surprise it turned out I was the lead – Miss Twentieth Century. Then I remembered how a lot of the men at the audition (there are always so many people at these things, looking at you and sizing you up) had kept smirking every time I went on about my period attributes. I suppose they'd already decided I was to be their Modern Miss.

This epic was filmed in some historic barn in the home counties. I sat on a throne on a dais in my best frock (we all had frocks in those days) while hordes of extras, all in various period costumes, cavorted round me. God knows what we were advertising, but it was shown quite a lot and I made a bit of money on the repeats. (This was before everything was automatically a "buy-out.")

At that time I was writing articles for Wheelers Magazine – a posh glossy put out intermittently by the restaurants (I presumed.) It paid extremely well (profits from the restaurants?) The editor was an ex-army officer, Anthony Wysard. He lived deep in rural country near Reading and I would occasionally be bidden to intimidating Sunday lunches there to "discuss ideas." It was some time after his death that I learnt my articles had brought in more offers of both further writing opportunities and acting work. It had been his private policy not to pass on any such offers to his contributors (!!!)

The next commercial I remember was one of the black spots of my life. Once again, I was the lead – a modern day young housewife – and the joke was I was hoovering the lawn. I wore the blue and white striped sailor dress from the Roy Plomley play "Double Crossing" that dear John Newbury loved so much. (It was on the tour that we met.)

But there I was, Little-Miss-Ever-Perfect-Housewife, hoovering the lawn of this suburban villa that was our location. And there was something else that even now I can't bear to think about. But it happened, and I saw it. And I had to hide every emotion of fear and horror that came over me, and get on with the job in hand.

During the day's filming, there were continual showers of rain and everyone had to rush for shelter. And – I really don't know why – the rest of the crew and directors were invited into the house where we were filming, doubtless with warm electric fires and welcoming cuppas. But I, the only cast member (yes, it was a solo performance) was forced to shelter in the garden shed, amid the old oil cans and rusted garden tools and unused lawn mowers. And there I shivered miserably, with only the drip drip of the rain for company, until filming recommenced. And I was unable to put the horror of what I'd glimpsed out of my mind.

The irony of all this is that about ten years later I chanced to meet the Casting Director who'd got me the job. "Oh Pamela," he said, "Do you remember that commercial where you hoovered the lawn?" (As if I'd ever forget.) "It won all sorts of prizes," he continued, "It was the Comedy Commercial of the year…"

This same Casting Director put me up for a commercial that I thought was for cat food in Milan.

By then, my first book, "Flavio and the Cats of Rome" had been successfully published and I really did show-off about it and successfully got the job. The flight out to Milan was a joy – a half-empty plane and I had a window seat to view the majesty of the Alps as we flew over. At Milan Airport, I met the young actor who was also in the commercial, and we were greeted by someone from the film company who offered us lunch. But we'd both eaten too much on the plane and could only toy with the salads much to the man's evident disappointment.

Then we were taken to the studios for costume fittings. A rather hideous purple dress awaited me, but it did fit. In the evening the director, Hamish Rothwell, took us both out to dinner. At least we were both hungry by then, and did full justice to the meal. We were put up at a very grand hotel – and for the first time I encountered those cards instead of keys. But the young actor was extremely chivalrous. He'd already carried my case, now he undertook the careful instructions of the key-card.

Early the next morning, we were whisked by car along what seemed a never-ending motorway to the studios. It was then that I learnt I hadn't come all that way to advertise cat food, but special dusters that picked up cat hairs. The principal actors were two extremely sulky looking long-haired Persian cats. We were assured they were specially trained. As they were far more important than us humans, it was decided they should be filmed first. Agog to watch their performance, I remained on the set. The cast were carried to their opening position by their trainer and her assistant. The lights were set, everything was ready, and Hamish called, "Action!"

Despite cooing noises from the trainer and the enticing tit-bits she offered, the cats didn't move. They sat motionless and thought about how they hated the world. Hamish tried for a second take. This time one of the cats yawned and the other began furiously washing its nether regions. The trainer suddenly spotted me crouched behind the sofa. "Pamela!" shouted the irate woman, "She distract my treasures. She must go!" So for many hours I was banished to my small dressing room. Luckily I had a good book. The day wore on and apparently the cats refused to do anything at all but sit and look glum which was their natural expression. As in all filming, time is money and Hamish was getting desperate. Pressed by the management, he decided to do all my scenes so that I could be put on a plane home that night.

Of course I knew the lines and the first scene was easy and all done in one or two takes. But at the end, I had had to have hysterics over my star cats, now banished to their dressing room. It had been a long day of waiting around, and somehow I found this difficult. Time was running out — "Pamela," said Hamish kindly, "Imagine your own cat being thrown out of the window." That did it for me. I instantly burst into tears and before I knew it, I was being applauded by the Italian crew. It's wonderful when it happens instantaneously like that. I remember my embarrassment when an eager young director on a film ordered the crew to clap me for just walking up a road.

But that was it – my Milanese commercial completed. Before you could say "Cat Dusters" I was dumped on a plane for Heathrow and I'd meant to say could I just have a glimpse of the Duomo before I left. But that had to wait some years for my wonderful trip with Alan and Marion. I suppose the cats were eventually persuaded to do something because it was finally completed and shown.

My agent then was lovely Simon Cutting. For some reason he couldn't explain, he had the most awful difficulty getting the payment for that commercial. The commercial was showing merrily in Italy, but they wanted to keep the money to pay Italian taxes. Simon sent them proof that I was a British taxpayer. No, that wasn't good enough. We had to produce some special form. Both Simon and I enquired everywhere for this. Some months later I did eventually run this elusive form to earth. On the same day, Simon phoned to say at last the money had come through.

But my favourite job of all time was when I did a commercial to be Madame Total Petrol in France. This ran for a whole year, and the six days spent making it were among the happiest in my life. I really only got the job through the intervention of my agent, Simon. On just this one occasion, he arranged for a woman friend of his to dress me for the audition. I remember being hustled into a wardrobe (where?) and bustled into an unaccustomed suit with a nipped in waist and a

Duchess of Windsor hat perched on my pinned-up hair. And thus attired, I got the part. They came to London for the casting because she was meant to be Finnish (blonde – see?) – the mother of a real alive and kicking Finnish racing rally driver. So successful was my get-up that the French company asked if I could bring the clothes with me. Luckily, the lady wasn't letting out these prize pieces from her personal wardrobe.

But they had a delicious (and much nicer) primrose yellow suit waiting for me, topped by a wide yellow hat. They gave me the hat when the filming finished, not alas the suit. The hat is in my wardrobe still, but I've never had occasion to wear it.

Since it was a petrol advert, my part largely involved driving a strange car. In France. On the wrong side of the road. At home, even after years of Mini owning, I know I'm not a good driver. In fact, when I get flustered or nervous, I'm extremely bad. But, although of course I'd never driven abroad before, and really never any cars except Minis, I took to it like a duck to water. Largely I think, because the director, Stéphane Clavier, was so lovely and had such faith in me. As an actress, he really thought I was Sarah Bernhardt. I could do anything with this belief he had in me and only made one mistake, making a right turn, in all the filming. And when that happened, Stéphane just laughed and stepped forward to hold up the traffic while I righted the car.

So for several happy days I drove through

fields studded with poppies below the Apennines. There was a long two to three hour lunch break, and all the crew and my lovely director and producer and my dresser and all the hair people, sat down at a long trestle table in a French orchard and had the most delicious meal. This was supplied by what was supposed to be the most famous outside catering unit in Europe. Stéphane said he had only one complaint about me – that was my inadequate French. Oh dear, despite much trying and effort, I've never been good at languages. Luckily, my part was mainly the driving and only a few words had to be spoken when I drew up at the Airport and met my son for the film, this real life racing driver. He hugged me emotionally and I felt we were friends for life.

But there had been one cloud on my horizon and that was during my first night in the hotel. At the time I got this lovely job, my mother had dementia. During the ten years of her affliction the rest of the family simply turned a blind eye and left me to struggle with all the problems that come with this most distressing disease. I was her full-time carer. Obviously she couldn't be left but I needed the money the job would bring and I wasn't going to let such a golden opportunity slip. So I decided to ask my brother (who lives in Wiltshire) to look after Marje for the week. I felt no guilt or hesitation in asking since he'd offered no help – either financially or physically – with our mother's illness. It was a burden I'd borne entirely alone. So I rang, and got his wife, Mary. Peter was out. Mary immediately vetoed her husband coming up to look after Marje while I was away. But I persisted. I always remember her saying," Are you going to make a habit of this – like every month?" I assured her it was a once in a lifetime opportunity. So I flew off to France and Peter was to come later to my London flat to look after his mother.

With the flight and everything, it had been a long day. I was half-asleep when, at midnight, the phone rang in my hotel bedroom. "A call for you – Madame," said the French operator. "No, no, it can't be. A mistake," I whispered, but already could hear Peter's agitated voice on the other end of the line. It seemed that ever since his arrival at the flat, shortly after my departure, Marje, convinced he was a strange man who had come to rape her, held him at bay at the end of a bread knife. Neither of them had even sat down for many hours.

I was furious. White with anger. It was Peter's own fault. He hadn't been near us for years. Marje didn't know him. No wonder she thought he was a stranger. And how dare he worry me in a way that could be so detrimental to my work when, as I told him, there was nothing I could do about the situation. "Worry belong you! I'm hundreds of miles away and cannot help," I said firmly, replacing the receiver. Later I gathered he then rang his wife, who came up to London on the milk train. Once there was another woman in the flat, albeit a stranger, my mother settled down and although keeping them both at a distance, the six days were passed without further incident.

238

I managed not to let this unfortunate incident cloud my happiness over the next few days. We weren't going to film on the Monday, I gathered – it was a Bank Holiday in France. So I began to plan for my free day.

A Japanese member of the crew – I was never sure what he actually did (there are always so many people in film units – on commercials you hardly have time to get to know them all.) Anyway, he asked me in perfect English if I would like them to hire a car for me for the day, "So that I could explore the region." I nearly fainted on the spot – doing the driving for the advert was one thing – I really only had to get from A to B, with the other traffic held up for me, and a clear road, but to set off in a strange car in a strange country, on my own, was too horrific even to contemplate. He seemed a bit disappointed when I refused his kind offer.

I set out, on foot, to explore the town, and the first thing I met was a large flock of sheep. Half the population seemed to have turned out to see them. Or was it because it was a Bank Holiday? Then it dawned on me that they were on the way to the abattoir – and they would be lamb chops on the nouvelle cuisine at my grand hotel. I racked my brains (I used to try so hard in French. We had a lovely teacher, Miss Rickman, but I was never any good at languages.) Scraping my memory, I came out with, "Où va les moutons?" A kindly woman, with an overflowing basket, patted my arm, and explained in perfect English that the sheep were bound for their summer pastures high in the mountains and yes, the townsfolk did turn out every year to watch them going. I was so relieved and waited until the last sheep was out of sight and then found a little café by the market and a satisfying café au lait.

Then I set out for what I'd guessed would be quite a walk along a dull main road. But I eventually reached my goal – the asylum where Van Gogh sent himself, and where he ate his tubes of paint on the bad days and painted some of his greatest pictures on others. I walked up the drive, it was May and too early for the irises, but I pictured them as they must have been when, on his saner days, he walked out to paint in the surrounding cornfields, all those pictures, which no one in the world wanted, and all he could do was send them to his brother Theo, until he lost all hope.

The hotel where I was put up was really so very grand I found it all a bit overpowering. One day, I saw Barbara Cartland sitting on the terrace. You couldn't miss her – she was dressed in shocking pink from her wide hat down to her matching shoes. The night after the incident with my brother, I'd crept down to the dining room for dinner as I'd been instructed. Alone in the vast crowded room, lit by many chandeliers and with at least three waiters vying for my attention, I was completely overawed by the whole set up. I didn't understand most of the things on the menu, and hadn't the faintest idea what to order. So I kept pointing at various things in an infantile kind of way. Fearing the wine waiter would have a heart attack if

I asked for "eau," I did procure a bottle of red wine and had one glass. It probably cost more than I was getting for the whole commercial – the courses, when they came, were tiny. I supposed they were nouvelle cuisine. All the other tables were full of chattery French people but I felt they were giving me, sitting alone, many curious glances.

My embarrassment was so great that the next night I decided I couldn't face the horrors of the dining room and would just stay in my room. With the magnificent location lunches we had, I wasn't at all hungry. And I had a bag of toffees with me I'd brought from home as a comfort rag. But that night the producer came up to my room to see me about something or other. He was as lovely as Stéphane, and very soon he asked me if I had dined. I immediately said no, thank you, I wasn't hungry. He sat beside me on the bed and reached for the menu that was hiding under the telephone. "Pamela, I think you should eat something – you are working very 'ard, you know – you use a lot of energy in your work. I order Room Service. I think – let me see, perhaps you like – and this – and this." He picked up the telephone and there was a lot of French I didn't understand. Then, after thanking me for all my good work on the film (and how wonderful they all thought I was!) he left me. A little while later a most delicious and delicate meal was brought to my room. And for every other night of my stay, too.

I believe the commercial was very successful and Madame Total Petrol ran for a year. The following year, by a strange chance, my agent's partner, Hugh, succeeded me, and went out to film as Monsieur Total Petrol. I gathered he, too, had a wonderful time. "But Pamela," he told me, "they couldn't stop talking about you. As if you were Sarah Bernhardt or something. I really got sick of hearing about how wonderful you were!" D'you wonder this was one of my most favourite jobs ever?

I don't think Harry Hill's name was mentioned when I went for the audition. I just know I had a casting in Camden Town and with some difficulty I located the Gas & Electric Co. It seemed I had come at the wrong time – I arrived in the morning, I was expected in the afternoon. But they agreed to see me, and I sat in the waiting room with a lot of young girls. One had come from Scotland and the others, variously, from the North. It seems accommodation in London is so pricey now, it's cheaper for these aspiring youngsters to live at home and travel these vast distances to come up to London for auditions.

My turn came, and I was ushered into a small, crowded room. A lot of men seemed to be looking at me. The first question was – "Did I enjoy the Harry Hill Show?" Realising to admit I can't wait to turn it off would bring the whole proceedings to a halt, I assured them I loved Harry Hill and found him so funny and amusing! (May God forgive me – but a job is a job.) The next request was something of a shock too. One of the men leant forward and said, "Dance!"

"Dance?" I said vaguely, looking round the room. There wasn't much room between the desks. And some music – heaven knows what it was – was switched on. Not for nothing had I been toiling weekly to the Gabrielle Roth Five Rhythms dance class at the Mary Ward Centre. I danced; and then went home to my cat and a cup of tea.

A few days later my agent phoned to say I'd got the job. She seemed unclear as to exactly what it entailed – except that I was going to dance. I pressed for further details – *what* exactly was I going to dance? Jackie asked what the music had been at the audition. Of course I hadn't the faintest idea. All she knew was that it was one day's filming, at a meagre fee. "But I've got you a car!" she added triumphantly.

So on the appointed day, the usual very grand limousine whisked me away somewhere in the direction of Heathrow. We ended up in some sort of Industrial Estate. Neither I nor the driver knew exactly where I was to go, so in the end I thanked him and got out of the car, clutching my bag. I wandered about between business units and vast echoing empty studios. Eventually, I met a man who took me to a woman, who took me to where I was supposed to be. No one seemed to be expecting me, and I was put to wait in a wardrobe crammed with rather smelly old clothes.

At last I was taken to make-up. The lady was nice and did my face very well. It seemed I was to be a 50's "Beatnik" fan of Harry Hill. I was assured the look was to be glamorous. I'd already murmured about my make-up allergies, but all was going well until fake eyelashes were produced. "I don't think I'll be able to wear those," I faltered. But the glue was applied and one set of lashes pressed into place. Immediately, my eyes erupted – tears poured down my face, making mud of the lady's earlier work. I must say she took it very well (lucky I'd mentioned about the allergies) and satisfied her pride with loads of black mascara instead of the falsies.

Then on to wardrobe. A not quite so nice lady scoffed at the clothes I'd so carefully brought with me, as directed, following a phone discussion about what I should wear. They'd got me a beatnik hat, and a fifties jacket and skirt. I supposed it would look all right. I was taken to the floor where the shooting was actually taking place. There was the fat girl from Scotland – I was glad she'd got the job – wearing a bright pink jumpsuit, jumping around singing.

They did take after take, and she apologised a lot, but she seemed very buoyant. Then I noticed Harry Hill had arrived. With that strange big collar he always wears, you couldn't really miss him. He was talking to the man who'd ordered me to dance at the audition – who I took to be the director. Harry Hill kept giving furtive sideways glances in my direction. Then they came over to me – so I was formerly introduced. "This is Pamela," said the director – like I was a rabbit he'd produced out of a hat. Harry Hill shook hands very nicely – of course he was once a GP. I wondered what it would have been like to be one of his patients? They quickly withdrew – there was no further conversation.

It was a long time before the big girl in pink got her song in the can. Then it was my turn. I'd asked the director to tell me exactly what he wanted me to do. "Just do what you did at the audition!" he almost snapped. Somewhere along the way I'd gathered I was supposed to be performing a 50's jive. I'd rushed out and bought a Cliff Richard CD of "Happy Holiday" and I'd done quite a lot of prancing round the flat to that. The music started and there was Harry Hill gyrating, dead centre, in front of the camera. So I gyrated too, but keeping a respectful distance, since after all, he was a Big Star. But he was having none of that. "Come over here, come to me," he urged, in a piercing whisper. So I grew bolder, and hopped and bopped at him – even presenting him with my butt from time to time.

Then it was the director's turn – he was almost screaming, "Here! Here! In front of the camera," so I obliged. I moved centre, and I danced, I wiggled. I thought it was never going to end. I believe we did it for about eight minutes (of which about 3 seconds were used.) And then Harry Hill started to clap me, and everyone on the set followed suit and applauded. Someone brought me a cold drink, and the man playing the Susan Boyle lookalike said, "You've set the bar very high for the rest of us."

I was told to wait, as I might be needed again. It was interesting watching the rest of the filming. Harry Hill did some of his stuff – throwing a rag doll – meant to be a baby – into the crowd. The audience screamed with laughter – why do they find this funny, I wondered?

Then a vast trampoline was wheeled onto the set. I was asked if I'd like to have a go on it – in character? By now the adrenalin was running high and I was game for anything and readily agreed. But soon the announcement came over the tannoy, "Pamela is not to go on the trampoline. It's a wrap for her." So I shed the beatnik hat and the 50's clothes and another smart car took me home. And that was the end of my day's filming, I thought.

Before Christmas my agent told me she'd heard they were going to use my dancing in Harry Hill's commercial for his new album. This meant that financially my day's film money should become something very different. My agent departed to join her family in France for the festivities. No one seemed to know anything at all about my Harry Hill job. It wasn't until well into the New Year that I really learned about the commercial. In the middle of January I managed to speak to the PA at Gas & Electric on the phone. She said yes, my dancing had been used (and was very good) she added. But the commercial – for Harry Hill's new album – had only been shown for three weeks, and now it was finished. I said I hadn't seen it, and she said, "You don't watch enough TV, Pamela!"

Now that I knew for sure my dancing had been used in the commercial, I got onto my agent again, and complained bitterly that the £100 I'd received for one day's filming was certainly not what

I should get now we knew it had been used in the commercial. (And without us being told.) She said she'd look into it.

Eventually, she rang and said she'd talked to Douglas Rye, who'd engaged and directed me, and Nicci Topping, the casting lady. They were both so sorry, yes, there had been a lot of muddle and confusion, and of course I should have been paid more. But, alas, there was now no more money! They each sent me an apology. My agent added that I now had two alternatives – I could take them to Equity – with extremely severe repercussions for both of them, or I could trust to their honour and good nature that they would think of me for future work, and re-employ me as soon as they could. I chose the latter. And, of course, I've never heard from Miss Topping or Mr. Rye ever again. More fool me!

CHAPTER SEVENTEEN

Famous people who've crossed my path

1955 – 2015

Roger Moore

During my acting life I've come across one or two film stars: the first was Roger Moore. I managed to get a really good little part in the film "Crossplot," directed by the distinguished Alvin Rakoff. My scenes were all in the church of a picturesque village in Hertfordshire. I was a little country girl getting married to the now well-known screen actor David Bradley (famous for his rather gormless face.)

The film was of the spy-thriller genre, and of course Roger Moore was the Bond guy catching the Baddies. I never fully understood the intricate plot, and now I've forgotten why, but at the "has anyone any just impediment?" in my marriage ceremony, Roger Moore stood up and said loudly from the back of the church, "Yes, there is." Cue a very nice crying scene for me.

As we were filming, we all had hours and

hours of hanging about doing nothing. These were passed in the Unit Base in the Village Hall. Roger Moore was always there – I wonder why he didn't have his own trailer (perhaps there wasn't parking room – it was a very small village?) The star was very pleasant and friendly and said lots of nice things to me. He was very complimentary about my wedding dress – I was thrilled with my cozzie. I'd been treated like a real bride, and taken to a specialist shop in Oxford Street and allowed to choose for myself. Feeling as if I was getting married for real, I chose a very simple full length dress that really suited me. In the film, after bringing my wedding ceremony to an abrupt halt, Roger made a quick getaway in a scarlet Mini. (I drove out to the location each day in my first light blue Mini – "Eyr," giving a lift to Anthony Sharp, who played the presiding vicar.) I couldn't believe the speed with which Roger accelerated away, and, in one of our long waits, begged to know how it was done. Roger spent a long time explaining and demonstrating this trick but I've never mastered it. You need to have the car ready in gear and then you just jam down the accelerator. I guess my legs aren't strong enough. But thanks to Roger, making "Crossplot" was fun.

Sean Connery

I worked with Sean Connery on the television production of "The Crucible" for Granada, and filmed in Manchester. Susannah York was also in the production, her first starring rôle, as she made sure we all knew. I played Susanna Walcott, another of the young girls. I had rather unhappy memories of Manchester – I'd gone up there to both rehearse and record another TV series, "The Runnable Stag." This was to be in six episodes, and I was in nos. 2 – 5. When I arrived on the appointed date, I was told there'd been trouble with the juvenile girl, and they were going to do episode one all over again. "Right," I said. "I'll go back to London for the week." "Oh no," said Granada, "You can't do that. You've got to stay in Manchester." (I think they added, "in case we need you.") But they did say, "If you're not here, you won't be paid."

So there I was, stuck in Manchester for a week, knowing no one, not welcome at the Granada Studios, on bed and breakfast terms only at my hotel, and at a complete loss as to how to fill my days. It was November, and fog enclosed the city, so no outdoor excursions. I spent long hours in the Kardomah Café, saw "Rin Tin Tin" twice, and "Passion Flower Hotel" - desperately – four times. I wore out the floor at the Museum of Costume. In those days, that was all Manchester had to offer.

But for "The Crucible," mercifully, we rehearsed in London. One day, the great head of Granada, Sidney Bernstein, overheard our director, Henry Kaplan, using what he deemed "unseemly and inappropriate language." Henry (a Canadian) was suspended for a week, and his place was taken by the distinguished actor Noel Willman, already in the cast as Judge Danforth. Forbidding and ascetic, Mr. Willman made all us girls search for truth when he rehearsed us in our hysterical scenes. At one point we all had to turn icy cold, and he exhorted us to really feel it in our stomachs (he was not the sort of person to say "tummies.") Even now, when I come out of the Tavern in "Bohème" in Act III, I remember his words and where the cold first hits you.

We only went up to Manchester for the camera rehearsals and the transmission. When it was over, and safely "wrapped," several of us, including Sean, caught the midnight train back to London. We reached London in the small hours, and there was only one available taxi. We all piled in. There was Sean, myself, a black girl who'd been in the production, and her boyfriend who'd come to the station to meet her. We'd only gone a little way when these two started quarrelling. Soon their argument turned to fisticuffs. Sean grabbed my arm, rapped sharply on the partition glass, growled, "C'mon, Honey," and we were out of that cab faster than a cat swallowing a sardine.

Reader, I was alone with Sean Connery in the middle of the night, in the middle of North London (well, Mornington Crescent, actually.) All too soon, another taxi zoomed into view and we jumped in. Sean dropped me at my block of flats, kissed me briskly and said, "See you around, Honey." He drove off. I never saw him again until he was on the big screen as 007.

Roy Plomley

Surely everyone remembers the name Roy Plomley – the inventor and doyen of "Desert Island Discs" – that icon of Sunday morning broadcasting. That it's still going strong after all these years would have meant little to Roy – it was a bright idea he had one morning, and as far as he was concerned, that was the end of it. His consuming passion and interest were the plays he wrote. His burning ambition was to be a West End playwright. And the play of his that I was in so very nearly achieved that for him.

This play was called "Double Crossing" and had already been tried out, under many different titles, by various repertory companies. Roy had worked and reworked the script and felt it was ready to "go." We were to set out on a long tour, hopefully ending with the West End run he so much wanted. Roy came with the company on all the dates we played – constantly making notes, altering lines here and there, but always wonderfully encouraging to us, the cast. Roy proved himself to be the perfect travelling companion. If the cast are uncongenial, some tours can be a mini hell-on-earth. This one, with the beaming little bald-headed author popping up everywhere, was a veritable heaven. For a start, it was where I first met my dear friend John Newbury – a friendship that lasted so many years – I doubt I would have survived the Covent Garden accident without his almost daily help. Our friendship ended on Christmas Day 2012 when he suffered a serious stroke. Until the previous week he'd been playing one of the waiters in "Bohème." In our tour of "Double Crossing" he started off as the ASM, but in one of Roy's many rewrites he created the part of a young RAF Officer, and a thrilled John was asked to play him. I can't remember why the pilot was added to the plot. Possibly he rescued my elder sister, played by Jennifer Phipps, who was trying to swim the Channel. Act II was set in a small boat accompanying her attempt. It rocked only too realistically, causing the wonderful character actress, Joyce Barbour, who played Jennifer's coach, to call for a supply of Quells to be kept in the prompt corner. The lead was played by the then well-known American actor, Hartley Power. Jennifer and I were playing with American accents – I think Hartley was her Manager. He certainly wasn't our Dad. We were all rather in awe of him (except Joyce) on stage and off.

As well as Roy, the "Angels" or backers, the couple who were putting up the money for the production, travelled with us. The wife liked to have a finger in everything, but her speciality was costumes. As the younger sister, I had many changes, and she kept producing endless different dresses. I had to try them out at matinées. One week it was a fitted bright red frock. I pointed out that I would look like a moving pillar box. That number only lasted for the one performance. Finally, an enormously expensive rather nautical blue and white striped dress, complete with a sailor collar and full skirt (and underskirts) was purchased for me. It was one of the most flattering garments I've ever worn, and when the play closed the management gave it to me, and it remained in my wardrobe for years. John adored it and was always suggesting I wore it, but it was only suitable for "posh" occasions and not many of those came my way! My friendship with John blossomed, and as we played all those seaside resorts round the South coast, we seemed to go for endless walks together on the Downs in the afternoons.

After the show we would all adjourn to the nearest pub. Roy, standing drinks for everybody, would eagerly join in all the theatrical gossip. During our week in Eastbourne I had the misfortune to have digs right on the town's outskirts. At the end of the evening, Roy insisted on escorting me to my lodgings. I protested, assuring him I'd be OK. But Roy would take my arm firmly, saying, "We don't want to lose our Juvenile Lead," and we'd set off. They were some of the most interesting night walks I've ever had.

But it was our leading man, Hartley Power, that we lost. That week we were playing the end of the pier theatre in Brighton. And as he walked up those boards for the mid-week matinée he suffered a crippling heart attack (that ended his career, and very nearly, his life.) There was no question of his returning to the play. In those days Hartley was a big name and it was to this that Roy and the backers had pinned their hopes of a West End transfer. My old friend Norman Mitchell, the understudy, gamely stepped in and carried the show. But Norman would've been the first to admit he wasn't a "name." Norman always knew who was doing what in showbiz, and I used to ring him up when I was "resting" (the time when you really put in the hard work) and he would suggest people for me to pester with my job letters.

I believe there was a wild search for a star, or someone of similar status to take over the rôle, but no replacement was found. With Norman at the helm "Double Crossing" limped into Streatham Hill and Golders Green and sank without trace. Roy died, tragically and prematurely, only a few years later, and is now only remembered for "Desert Island Discs." Not as the famous playwright he so longed to be. He was one of the nicest people I've ever met.

Michael Winner

Everyone knew Michael Winner through his relentless publicity campaign of self-promotion: small, tubby, and tirelessly aggressive. We all knew his mother had squandered millions, but left enough for him to do the same. And he put quite a lot of it into making films. I got a small part in one of them – "Bullseye." I didn't meet him until the actual shooting – I got the rôle through the casting director. I was the Duchess of Syon and my first scene was in a tiny panelled bedroom at Hever Castle – home of the ill-fated Anne Boleyn. I didn't have time to explore – I was whisked down there, did the scene and back home again as soon as I had "wrapped." It was a modern thriller and I was dressed in a beautiful pink satin nightdress and a matching gown trimmed with swansdown. I sat on the edge of the bed, nervously awaiting the arrival of Mr. Winner. Eventually he swept in, followed by his entourage – at least ten people. He never went anywhere without such a bodyguard. I got up, and naturally went towards him to make my greeting. "Madame," he screamed, in that high nasal voice that became familiar through all those telly commercials (wasn't there something about a mouse?) "Don't move 'till I tell you to!" I subsided back on the bed. Winner did a lot of conferring with his aides and finally the 1st assistant director told me what to do. I remember there was a lot of parlaying about which hand I should use to turn on the radio. (It was the part of the plot that I heard something on the wireless.) So I did it, and the scene was done. Winner swept out without a word.

My second day on the film was altogether jollier. My drive out to Syon, in the suburb of West London, was exciting. It was very early in the morning and still dark, but Eyr, my first light blue Mini stormed along and I found a place in the car park. The 1st direction took me to make-up and Michael Caine said, "Mornin' Duchess." I wore the most beautiful dark green ball gown, my hair was up, and surmounted by a tiara. I met the Duke – my husband – played by a lovely actor and Henry Hall's son, James. Mercifully, I didn't have to speak in this scene, but James had a twelve line monologue to deliver. We were addressing our tenants (played by extras) in the great hall at Syon.

As the time for shooting the scene approached, Michael Winner appeared. He did everything possible to put James off – gibing him to dry etc. I gave my full silent attention to supporting my husband, who got through his speech faultlessly, and the whole scene was completed in a very few takes. Even Winner couldn't find anything to complain about. I was so proud of James. A friend of mine played a shepherd in the same film. With a flock of real sheep. During the shoot Winner gave the sheep instructions about where they were to go. When they didn't obey, he started kicking them. I think Michael Winner was one of the most unpleasant people I've ever met. I expect the sheep thought the same – until they met the man from the abattoir.

But I still sometimes go out to the Garden Centre at Syon to buy a few plants for my balcony. It's jolly to remember that once, for a short time, I owned the whole place.

Bernard Miles

I worked for Bernard Miles and his wife Josephine Wilson several times. I'd been writing to Bernard asking for jobs ever since I'd heard he was building the Mermaid Theatre. First he raised the money by giving performances in his own garden in

St. John's Wood. Then he appealed to audiences, the general public, anyone to "buy a brick." This scheme was so successful that he was able to build his wonderful theatre, hard by Bankside and the Thames, and all the places where Shakespeare had lived and worked. That the Mermaid is no longer used for anything connected with the theatre is a disgrace to the arts in London.

So, after many applications, Josephine finally auditioned me for one of her children's productions. These were intended for schools and gave two performances daily in term time. They were highly educational, but cleverly disguised as entertainment. Apparently there was a vacancy in the regular cast and I'd been suggested. Mr. Miles was friendly and charming, though I later discovered Josephine was the power behind the throne and often told Bernard exactly what should be done. She asked all the usual questions, and then came the one I'd been dreading, "You can sing?" As I've previously mentioned and as Mark Twain put it, "As a singist I am not a success." So I demurred, and Josephine persisted. "But you're all right singing hymns with other people?" I nodded dumbly and the job was mine.

The first programme I did was about electricity. I don't remember much about it, except eager kids rushing up onto the stage joyfully giving each other electric shocks. With a morning show and a matinée it was quite demanding work. I first met David Rowley, who became a dear friend. He played the piano for the shows and reinforced the singing, as we all, a company of six, bawled out the songs that repeated the educational message of the show.

The next one I did was about Hearing. There was a huge model of a human ear on stage, big enough for me to creep inside. I had a long, long monologue pointing out all the different parts and their functions. As I finished, I had to jump out of the ear very quickly and hop onto the revolve. At one matinée I broke my foot doing this. I think I was getting a bit tired. Someone took me to A&E at Bart's and they strapped it up. I was back for the show the next morning.

Bernard Miles took a great interest in the Ear Shows. Or rather, at that time, he was showing a great interest in me. He would waylay me in dark corners of the theatre (and there were many). He expected the odd kiss and told me I resembled the girl in Manet's "Behind the Bar." He assured me I would never be beautiful (I knew this only too well) but I was, like Trilby "jolie laide." He told me he was going to stage an adaptation of Henry James' "The Big House," under the title "The High Bid" and wanted me to play the young girl in this production. I suppose I was thrilled, but I'm sure I was sensible enough not to take this as a certainty.

I was feeling very unwell at the time, and had a terrible pain in my inside. But I duly turned up on the appointed day and auditioned for the "The Big House." Marje trailed behind me from London Bridge Station, carrying a bottle of brandy. It may have been the worst possible thing, but after the audition I really needed a drink.

The next day I was in St. Mark's' Hospital being operated on for an abscess in the bowel. I heard I'd got the part, but it meant nothing. The pain was so unrelenting there was nothing else in the world. You just have to grit your teeth and get on with it, and think of Louis XIV having his anal sphincter opened without anaesthetic, and getting up and going to meet with his Counsellors the same evening. After I was discharged a nurse came every day to dress the wound and gradually I got better. And I don't think I was unduly surprised when I heard I hadn't got the part after all, but was being offered the walking understudy.

I was still feeling fairly fragile when the rehearsals started. Soon I heard why the casting had been changed. Fenella Fielding, with all her wigs, was playing the lead. She was at the height of her fame, but so lacking in confidence she insisted on choosing her leading man. She also wanted young Janie Booth (who'd been at Chichester with her) to play the part I'd been promised. Bernard, meanwhile was determined the leading man should be that lovely actor Edward Woodward. Fenella wanted someone else. So a compromise was reached.

Bernard got Edward Woodward and Fenella got Janie Booth. I lost, and was banished to the understudy's room. But I wasn't in the least upset. I was still feeling a bit under the weather from the op. and I knew I wouldn't have been able to cope with the terrible rows among the cast that erupted almost daily. These were mainly between Bernard and Fenella, both steely characters with tempers to match. The other understudies were by far the nicest people in the company. We banded together and kept as far away from the storming principals as possible.

I consoled myself, if I had to be swapped, at least it was for a really good actor like Edward. And he was not only a wonderful actor, but a lovely person as well. Sometimes I thought he was the only sane one around. He tried to calm everything down, but with no success. Once "The High Bid" had opened, Bernard called meetings after the evening performances, which we all had to attend. We huddled in the auditorium, sometimes until one or two in the morning while Bernard and Fenella screamed and hurled insults at each other.

It was not an ideal convalescence. Our dressing room was our refuge, and we all prayed nightly that we wouldn't have to go on. Billy Russell, the old variety actor who played the ancient butler, sought refuge in our room when he wasn't on stage. He had a scene to himself in the play, where he wound and tinkered with all the clocks in the great house. He was an accomplished Music Hall artist, and knew how to play an audience. Invariably, his scene brought the house down, and he'd get a standing ovation. Fenella was furious because the play had received a cool reception from the critics. She tried to get Billy sacked. But Bernard, who had done variety himself, stood up for Billy and refused. More nightly rows. Billy would come to our dressing room saying what f**** they all were, and tell us stories about the past and people who were really talented.

A long time after "The High Bid" closed, I was accosted by Basil Ashmore as I was going home one night on the Underground. I had no idea who this strange man was. It seemed he had made the adaptation of Henry James' novel that we'd done at the Mermaid. This was all news to me. I'd never met him and knew nothing about him. He told me, in no uncertain terms, I'd only got into the production on his recommendation. I'd assumed I was in "The High Bid" through my sterling work in the Schools' productions, where Bernard had shown a great deal of interest in me. But no, it seemed this Mr. Ashmore had got me what, in the end, had been a rather lowly place in the company. My mind boggled. He seemed to think I owed him, but what exactly did he want? Money? Sexual favours? Luckily, my station came up. The tube doors opened and I stepped out into the night and never discovered any more about this unexpected and rather unsavoury confrontation.

Lord Kinnock

I had a fairly eventful journey to Wales for my day's filming on "Under Milk Wood." John Copley had given me an N/A for the performance of "Bohème" I was going to miss. The train I should have caught was cancelled, being on the next one I missed all the connections I should have caught. I kept calling the Fatti Film Office on my mobile. First of all Heather advised me to go on to Fishguard at the end of the line. But when I mentioned we'd just flashed through Port Talbot, she told me to get off at Swansea, where I'd be met.

So I got out and left the station and couldn't see anyone who looked remotely like Under Milk Wood. I bribed my way back onto the platform for a much needed pee. And waited. And then waited some more. I was finally picked up by someone from the film. And the actor playing Sinbad the Sailor got in the car too. He'd been on my train, but knowing the ropes, he'd adjourned to the nearest pub.

It was a long drive, all along the Gower Peninsula, and should have been a beautiful one, but the rain was pelting against the car window. But I didn't care – these people would take me to where I was supposed to be. I was finally dropped off at the prettiest little fairy-tale cottage in the fishing village of Solva. The Bavarian landlady was kindness itself, and after a visit to the Ship Inn (three doors down, where we were to film the following day) for some welcome supper, I passed a comfortable night.

In the morning I walked by the pretty harbour and took some photos before going in search of breakfast. This was provided by one of the Grips preparing for the day's filming. I found my way to the Costume Department at the back of the Ship Inn. I was kitted out in a 1940's cotton frock and a brown cardie. I tried innumerable pairs of shoes, all uncomfortable, and settled for a pair of "I've-been-milking" brogues, covered in mud. That I could barely walk in them didn't seem to matter – there were lots of chaps about with a willing arm to hang on to.

I was taken in a car up to the communal lunch in a building perched high on the cliff's edge at the top of the hill. I went down in the bus and joined the Extras. Many of them were dressed as famous people – Charlie Chaplin and Lloyd George, etc. Someone pressed a typed sheet into my hand and said, "Are you singing?" I looked at the paper, it was all in Welsh. But on the other side was a bawdy song in English, so I quickly learnt the words of the chorus.

Then we were told we were going to the Harbour for a practice. I found a ready arm and tagged along with the many instrumentalists, among them – a man with a serpent horn wound around his body and a girl with a double bass who told me she'd only been playing for a year. Neil Kinnock was there, having the busiest day of his life since stepping down from politics. Everyone wanted him in their Selfie, or his autograph. We went through the song a few times and then it was back to the pub for the actual filming. Dylan Thomas drank regularly in the Ship – Solva is quite close to Laugharne.

We were taken in one by one and given our places – I was told to sit in a corner and very soon, Neil Kinnock was put next to me. "You've met

Pamela?" said the 1st director, who was doing the arranging. The ex-politician gallantly kissed my hand and said, "I never forget a blonde" (we'd already been snapped together) and I said, under my breath, "actually, the hair's white."

For this big scene, Charlotte Church as Polly Garter, in check trews and a flowered top, came into the Inn parlour and bent down to the fireplace. Then she rubbed soot on the face of the nice man sitting on my left. Keith Allan, the director, came and explained that this was an old Welsh custom signifying that the magic was about to begin. The "magic" was us all roaring out the bawdy song which we did, many times over.

All the Welsh Rugby team, in their scarlet shirts, were in the pub, and I'm sure they were ready to join in the song with their lusty Welsh voices, but no one had given them the words. Everyone was representing a different facet of Wales and Welsh life. (I was there, having been in so many repertory productions of "Under Milk Wood.") Lord Kinnock couldn't believe I didn't know anything about Rugby. He spent the time between "takes" lecturing me about the noble game, and all the injuries he'd received playing it. I tried to introduce other subjects into the conversation. How was his wife, Glenys Elizabeth? I enquired. What were his children doing, I asked. But nothing would divert the ex-Labour leader from the topic of his favourite sport. By the time we were told the scene was a "wrap," and Neil had bawled out the song with the rest of us, and pretended to accompany himself on a miniature squeeze-box, I never ever wanted to hear 'Rugby' mentioned again.

I travelled back to London the next day with two of the press who'd come down to watch the filming of this epic scene. They were a bit cross as they'd meant to catch the same train as me. When it was cancelled, they'd gone off to have lunch somewhere and caught a later train. In total their trip to Pembrokeshire had taken nine hours. (Where had they been that I hadn't? I seem to have touched all stations between Paddington and the Gower Peninsula.) My trip of a lifetime had taken only seven hours – to join the magic of Dylan and all he stood for, and the joyous new film of "Under Milk Wood." Not to mention being chatted up by Lord Kinnock.

June Brown

To have known June Brown, National Treasure and doyen of "Eastenders," even briefly, is an honour. It was many years ago when we met – in a production of "The Way of The World" at the tiny Gate Theatre in Westbourne Grove. No one, except in the profession, had heard of June in those days. She was, like me, a struggling jobbing actress. The Gate was a shabby down-at-heel fringe theatre, but this production which Philip Mellor put on himself, was surprisingly illustrious.

Millament was played by Rachel Roberts, enjoying her new freedom – her marriage to Rex

Harrison had recently been dissolved. I'd seen her give many fine film performances, but all in modern scenarios. I don't think period plays, like the Congreve we were doing, were really her forte. But she kept us endlessly entertained as, in her lilting Welsh voice, she told us stories of how she and Rex always had a competition to see "who could be first out of bed to hit the bottle," and her most recent employment, which had been selling dog contraceptives. We were all short of funds in those days.

June was also a great raconteur, regaling us with stories of her large family and varied theatrical experiences. Her Mrs. Candour in "The Way of The World" was a perfect piece of period acting. But June was trained at the Old Vic School, and early in her career she played both Hedda Gabler and Lady Macbeth. I played Mincing, lady's maid to Millament, a small but perfect part for me. I felt very at home doing it, almost, as someone remarked, as if I'd been born to play her. I got the part because I knew Philip Mellor from my first job at the David Garrick Theatre, in Lichfield. Philip's wife, Jane, now busily engaged in child-rearing, had rather usurped my place as first ASM. She was tall, slim and pretty, and I had seen the few small parts that were going begging wouldn't be coming my way any more. So that was when I left and became the juvenile lead at Newcastle-Under-Lyme.

A few years later I chanced to meet June at an audition. She was still comparatively unknown but she instantly remembered me and recalled our time together at the Gate. In those pre-iPad days, we all lugged huge albums of our photos to castings. So a photo of me as the Black Mammy in "Rain" (which I did at Shrewsbury Rep.) would face my Amy in "Little Women," my party piece at so many different Reps. June immediately asked to look at my album. "Lovely photos you've got, darling," she said, the inevitable cigarette dangling from the corner of her mouth. "But d'you mind if I tell you something?" I nodded. Who would refuse a tip from June? She continued, "Wonderful pics you've got but where's your name? You should have it in big letters on every page. Emblazoned. Get it into people's heads, darling." Oh June, you were right of course. About so much.

I suppose now people will forget all the other wonderful work she did. She'll always be remembered as Dot Cotton in Eastenders, now almost the longest running character in British soap, for which she's received so many awards. In a way, it's a shame – she was such a great all-round actress (as well as a brave and generous human being.)

Personally, I like to remember her Nanny Slagg in the TV "Gormenghast." And also her appearance in the 2010 special "Strictly Come Dancing." I fondly remember her swearing lightly and praying through her clouds of cigarette smoke, that she would remember the steps. She danced the tango triumphantly. June herself is probably proudest of her MBE, awarded to her in 2009 for "Services to drama and charity." But I, along with most of the population of these islands, and beyond, will never forget the episode of Eastenders she carried so triumphantly on her own. One long uninterrupted thirty minute monologue. One of the most moving performances ever on TV. Was there a dry eye with anyone who watched the tour-de-force that June Brown gave that night?

John Betjeman

I was still very young, but nevertheless, I felt insulted when BBC TV rang up and offered me this job as an "extra." Luckily, I swallowed my pride and accepted. That day proved to be one of the most wonderful and instructive of my whole career. I was to be a Victorian housemaid in one of those big old mansions in Melbury Road, West London. A house once owned by a great collector, one of the Pre-Raphaelites, I think. And the programme was a live documentary hosted by John Betjeman. He was going to stay on the ground floor and talk to the camera, explaining the treasures of the house to the viewers. And I was going to scamper up and down the stairs – it was a tall, narrow house with three floors, and point to the antiques as the Poet Laureate described them.

Of course I'd read, and loved, his poems. When I was introduced to him in the morning – we rehearsed all day – he was even more charming than I'd expected. "Betj" as I learnt his friends called him, with his shy smile like a schoolboy caught doing something he shouldn't. His smile widened (his teeth were *very* crooked) and he announced himself enchanted with my "get-up." My hair had been put in a high bun, supporting a small, very starched, white cap. A long black dress, lace at the collar and cuffs (it was a very affluent house,) a frilly apron, and, under the dress, a saucy bustle, which, as the day progressed, received more and more pats from "Betj."

All day I scampered up and down the stairs, followed by a man with a hand camera. When I did touch base, there was John B. almost crying with delight at the way the "pictures" were coming up on his monitor. He never failed to congratulate me, and made many helpful suggestions. He was as huggable as a teddy bear. Behind the frequent dithering cries of "Oh, my! Oh, my!" was a mind as acute and sharp as forked lightning. This had propelled him from his, as he thought, humble middle class origins, to be a friend of Royalty (Princess Margaret was a devoted admirer) and all the Aristocracy, and the Recognised Rescuer of Old Buildings and the only Post Laureate to become a bestseller. He was once heard to murmur that he loved all Piers, whether they were at the seaside or in the Palace of Westminster.

His great knowledge of the history of antiques left me speechless. He had no script – all that day he poured out – extemporising – all this knowledge, never for one second appearing to "dry." And if anything was technically wrong, he was onto it in a flash. But to get what he wanted he approached the lighting expert, or whoever it was, with his diffident charm – "I've just noticed – now of course I don't know about these things, but might it not be better if…" And whatever it was, would be smilingly altered to meet his complete approval. People loved John. There was one Greek vase I had to point out and it showed several couples – well, you can guess… As I set off up the stairs I heard him murmur, "I do love a bit of decadence. Livens everything up."

During the afternoon I was despatched down to a pitch dark cellar in the basement. (Not followed by my faithful cameraman.) After some searching about with a very small torch (all the Beeb could provide.) I emerged triumphantly with a dusty bottle of some very old claret. It was to feature in the programme, and John treated it with almost religious reverence. After we'd wrapped, he broke it open and I was allowed a sip. After all the glowing adjectives that had been ascribed to it in the programme, I thought it tasted of nothing but dead leaves. But I'm no connoisseur.

Just before we went on air, the director realised there were a couple of extra minutes of talk needed. John immediately suggested an object on the top of the bookcase close to his mark. (He stood for the entire programme.)

I was summoned, but this small statue was far beyond my reach. "Quick! Quick! Something she can stand on," urged John. A pouffe was produced and I jumped up onto it. John clapped his hands with delight. "Oh you dear thing – would you do that again, just for me?" Bustle-a-wagging, I bobbed on and off the pouffe, and the Poet became almost transcendent with delight. The floor manager began to count down the minutes, and we did the programme. A day I shall never forget.

Ken Russell

When I heard Ken Russell had died, I was sad he'd been so neglected in his later years. OK, so some of his work was mad and bad, but he did make some very good films. And I was – just – in one of the good ones: "Savage Messiah." Even at that age I didn't do "walk-ons," but I'd agreed to be an extra on that, because the film was about Henri Gaudier-Brzeska, the young French sculptor who was killed early in the First World War. Ever since reading Christopher Ede's book (of the same title,) he'd been one of my heroes. Though back then I'd seen very little of his work – maybe the odd thing at the V&A. Years later I made a special expedition to Kettle's Yard in Cambridge and at last saw a lot of his work – etchings, prints and sculptures. I particularly remember a little round curled-up Dachshund that I would gladly have put in my pocket.

So there I was, being an extra on this film starring Dorothy Tutin as Sophie, Brzeska's devoted girlfriend. On one of my two days work I overheard her being extremely stroppy with the 1st assistant. She wanted time off from filming to get her hair done. He seemed unwilling to grant this but I bet she got what she wanted. In those days she was at the top of the theatrical tree. Yet I believe she had a very sad end, if the film Virginia McKenna made about it is to be believed – dying of dementia in an uncaring NHS home.

I'd had a very encouraging costume fitting with Shirley Russell, Ken's first wife. She collected vintage and period costumes and was thrilled that I was so tiny. (In those days, I was still smoking twenty Senior Service a day.) Her delight knew no bounds when she found I could wear a genuine 1920's black lace cocktail dress she'd had for ages but couldn't find anyone who would fit into it. She was delighted it was at last going to be used in a film.

So there I was, suitably clad, mooching about with lots of other extras in the Vortex Nightclub scene. I remember Ken's face being very red – he seemed to find us all exasperating. (I expect we were – his directions were quite hard to follow.) His hands would shoot Heavenwards, as if asking for divine guidance in getting just what he wanted from the idiots. Then, with a despairing shrug of the shoulders, he left the scene in the more than capable hands of the 1st assistant. But he soon returned and resumed his place behind the camera, shouting even more complicated directions.

After my two days' work, the scene was finally wrapped. I stood in a queue and collected my pitiful money (extras weren't so well paid in those days) and prepared to go home. The door of the dingy dressing room, where all the female Night Clubbers had been herded together, was thrown open. The 1st assistant, in a state of great agitation, burst in. One or two of the girls, not yet changed, covered themselves modestly with towels. "Who? Who was...?" began our male intruder. Then he saw Shirley's little black dress on the rail where I'd carefully hung it. (Extras don't get dressers.) He pounced on it with a sigh of relief. "Who wore this?" Sheepishly I half raised my hand. "Would you step outside for a moment?"

I followed him into the corridor. He asked my name and telephone number, and transferred the info. to his clipboard. What had I done? "Ken's spotted you!" he announced in tones suggesting I was to be Queen of the May. I didn't say anything and let him continue. "He was very pleased with what you did in the Vortex today. He's offering you a bit part. A real part, in the next scene. It'll be another two day's work. Starting tomorrow."

I waited quite a long time before I said, "No thank you." I thought he was going to have an apoplectic fit. "But pet, Ken's spotted you. It's a great honour." It was like the words were in italics. But at home I had my mother with a sprained ankle, needing to be waited on, hand and foot. And the cat was sick, too. So I said, "no" again.

But in Ken Russell's world, refusals didn't happen. Didn't exist. I was cajoled, pleaded with, coerced (and I must say, I enjoyed it) and was even offered a bit more money (that was great.) I finally agreed to present myself for a 5am call the next day.

I made my way home from the studios, somewhere at the top of Ladbroke Grove. I fed and watered my mother, and reported on the events of the day. The cat had been violently ill, so I had to scrub the kitchen floor. Ruefully thinking Dorothy Tutin wouldn't have to do anything like that. (How did I know?) I set the alarm clock for three thirty.

And all these years later, I realise it was a great honour. Thank you, Ken.

CHAPTER EIGHTEEN

2006

It came as a complete surprise when, on one of my routine visits to Mr. Groom's clinic, he suddenly announced that my leg had set and I could have the Ilizarov frame removed. At once I protested, but it was difficult to explain my fears. I tried to tell Mr. Groom of the horror I'd felt when my leg broke under me in the road, after St. Thomas' had assured me it was completely set. How could I be certain the same thing wouldn't happen again?

I think, at last, he understood; and it was agreed I should wear the hated contraption for one more month "for safety's sake." But before the magic date of the removal, I had many other problems to solve. I was so frightened of my new leg (as it would be) re-breaking, that I decided that I simply couldn't risk the fifty stairs up to my flat. Luckily Denville Hall had a room and were prepared to look after me for three weeks' convalescence. This time, with the compensation looming, I elected to pay. On my previous visits I'd been supported by the Actors' Benevolent Society, to whom I owe a deep debt of gratitude and my grateful thanks. Denville even seemed to think it was quite a good idea I was looked after for this interim period.

Then there was the question of transport. I couldn't have my usual ambulance because I wouldn't be returning home. There's a maddening NHS rule you must be delivered back to where you've been picked up from. This greatly inconveniences people trying to continue with their work, who go on to their place of business after their appointment at the Clinic. So – no ambulance. But lovely John Newbury volunteered to drive all the long journeys that would be involved.

On the appointed day, John picked me up in his large old car. Our journey was pretty hazardous; John had no idea where Denmark Hill was. As my ambulances had always taken different routes, I was pretty vague too. Also John had to be careful not to stray into the congestion zone, that would have cost us a fortune. So many hasty U-turns were executed, gales of laughter from John, nail biting for me. But we arrived at King's safely and John dropped me off and went in search of the elusive and highly priced parking. By now I was quite nimble at hopping on my crutches, but today everything was different. Instead of joining the long queues for x-rays (that would come later) I was directed straight to Sister Debbie. I didn't have to wait long. Soon she was helping me onto the table in a screened-off alcove. There was no nonsense about Debbie. "Usually it's the men who scream," she observed, putting on her rubber gloves. Of course there was no anaesthetic. Debbie pulled out the pins that had been piercing my bones, swiftly and dexterously, one by one. And mopped up the drops of blood as she moved down the leg. When she'd finished, I stared down at my bare leg. It looked like a white caterpillar grub that doesn't know where it's going. Debbie carefully put the other slipper I'd brought with me on my right foot and, with the utmost gentleness, helped me off the table. She held out my crutches – I grasped at them for support. Debbie laughed. "Try putting your foot on the floor. It'll bear your weight, I promise..." I left the room with a sort of hobbling limp. My right leg didn't seem to like the idea of walking at all. It felt very strange indeed, but the x-rays reinforced the soundness of the bones. Back in Mr. Groom's office, he was anxious to photograph my new leg. Of course I gave my permission, and I was glad he was so pleased with his handiwork. But to me, having both my legs working just felt so strange. The 'good-byes' and 'thank-yous' were said, and there was John jangling his car keys and beaming as usual. He wanted to make a start on the next part of our long journey.

I regret to say I didn't even try to walk properly to where the car was parked, but went back to using my crutches in the old familiar way. John proceeded to drive across and around London and out the other side to Northwood. He'd had a sandwich, and there was one waiting in the car for me. Without any mishaps we arrived at Denville Hall. Mrs. Miller was there to greet me, remarking that we were at least two hours earlier than she'd expected. Several of the staff were in the hall, and they all embraced me warmly. Much to my relief, I was put straight into a wheelchair. Then we went up to my not very attractive room. It was long and narrow, with hardly room for the wheelchair. It was in the new block that had been built since my last visit. A lavish tea was brought up, but John hardly ate anything, he was anxious to begin his long journey home. We had a quick embrace for all his tireless support throughout that long day. And he was gone. But we'd be meeting before very long.

Again and again I thanked my lucky stars that I'd decided to start my new life with the help and support Denville provided. They urged a slow and steady start to learning to walk again. For some days the wheelchair was allowed in the dining room for meals and every day my leg seemed to grow stronger and my confidence grew. Mrs. Miller even arranged some aromatherapy for me. "I thought it would be comforting," she said mildly. It was wonderfully relaxing.

So the date for my final homecoming was fixed. John was busy, so I was going to have a private ambulance, which was going to be very expensive. Roll on the compensation. I was helped into the ambulance and sat in the sitting up seat like the recovered person I was. Many of the Denville staff were there to wave me off. For safety's sake my crutches were put in beside me. It surprised me that the hospital refused to take them back, apparently disinfecting them for re-use was costly and impractical!

So I was walking now, albeit very slowly. I turned the key in the downstairs front door. Fifty stairs faced me. I put my left foot up, and dragged my right one up to join it. It took a long time to reach my flat. There was no one to welcome me, but dear Michael had been in and put some food and milk in the fridge. No carers now. My new adventure – living a normal life, was just beginning.

The next morning my elderly physiotherapist came to see me. She was pleased and surprised at the progress I'd made. She said she had a young boy she was training who would accompany me on walks until I was fully independent.

This nice lad came several times, and I practised walking up and down the road. We even made it round the corner to the pillar box where my leg had broken under me – it seemed such a long time ago. "Granny" as I privately called my old physiotherapist (she was just about to retire) phoned, and said she thought I was ready to go on a bus. The Boy would, of course, come with me.

So the next day we made it to the station, and slowly, slowly across the zebra. The Boy held his hand up professionally to halt the oncoming traffic. When the bus came, he reached to help me, but I managed to haul myself on board. Luckily the driver didn't start until we were safely seated. I was nearly sick with expectation, I'd waited more than three years for this. "Will we – " I was so excited I could hardly get the words out, but I managed it at last, "Will we be able to go to Smiths?" The boy nodded. "And buy pens and a notebook?" The boy seemed to think this was strange, but he nodded again.

We reached Notting Hill. I allowed myself to be helped off the bus. We crossed the road and I made it up the kerb, I walked slowly, but I was walking towards Smiths.

CHAPTER NINETEEN

What happened next; or
it was never on my bucket list
to fly to the Ukraine

2015

So I walked, albeit with a limp. If only I'd been able to see the future, and all that the coming years held, and the amazing things that would come my way in my eighties. There was the occasion I was given a pink, faux fur coat (as well as being paid) for filming. This was bought as a cozzie, but wasn't used, despite my longing glances, during the day. Mostly I was dressed in combat gear or fatigues. I've no idea why, especially as the filming was of dances for people wearing hardly anything at all.

As the "good-byes" and "thank-yous" were being said, I expressed one last appreciation of the pink coat. Whereupon the producer rushed to fetch it and pressed it into my arms: "Please have it! We're so delighted with what you've done today!" So the pink faux fur coat is hanging in my wardrobe. I sometimes wear it as a dressing gown. But out...?

Oh, I don't know...

And then there was the Mastercard commercial, which I completed after four hard days filming in Vienna. (How can filming be described as "hard"? We're waited on hand and foot. It's not coal-mining). I had a free morning before the plane back to London, and the stout German dame who directed the action asked my make-up lady what I most wanted to see? This lovely lady said she knew Pamela had hoped to see the Spanish Riding School – but there was no performance that Monday morning. Whereupon, Mr and Mrs Mastercard, who'd been so critical during the filming, waved their magic wand, and a private visit was arranged for me, just as if I was the Queen. Of course I went to thank the Sergeant-Major who was responsible for my treat. She jumped to attention and barked, "Pamela, you earnt it!"

I was shown all over the Riding School, and met the famous grey stallions in their own stables. (And there's always one bay in residence – "for luck".) Of course, it's verboten to touch these magic horses (germs!) but one friendly fellow managed to nibble the shoulder of my coat, before being sternly reprimanded by his groom. The visit was one of the most wonderful happenings of my life, only to be equalled, perhaps, by Domingo kissing me after our very last "Bohème."

I went back into "Bohème", there hadn't been a revival while I was 'off'. Pauline and I were retired, we became the Elegant Ladies in the Café Momus. But in 2015 the Gent with the Scythe tried to fell me again – with three attacks of cramp each lasting over three hours. My right leg was left even more permanently twisted.

But after the cramp St. Mary's Hospital threw me out, saying they could do nothing for me. Jackie, my new agent, promptly got me into a big film "Level Up" as a Housekeeper in a strange brothel, filmed in one of those big houses in Portland Place. Ironically, there was a real brothel on the floor above. The leading man, Josh Bowman, was great fun, and we laughed a lot, especially when I found a pile of blue magazines in the hall we were using as part of the set.

Someone asked how I'd morphed from an extra at the opera to being a film star. As I'd been, or was, neither, I just laughed. Then, by self-submitting, followed by pressing emails and a collage-card I made myself, I got a day on the new "Under Milk Wood" film; described elsewhere in this book.

In 2015 there was the very last revival of "Bohème". I was only able to do it because poor Jenny Thorne had died. I took her place in the sitting-down rôle of Madame Momus. The last night alone made it worth the humiliation of having to hire cars to the theatre, and being lifted into my seat behind the reception desk. The Telegraph were kind enough to print an article I wrote about forty-one years in the opera, and Domingo kissed me as he crossed the stage after conducting. (I felt I'd been kissed by God!) There was a party for John Copley, though I couldn't understand why he wasn't given a leaving present after his wonderful years of service at the Opera House.

But 2016 was _my_ year, the year I really came into my own as a character actress.

I was so keen to see the Queen, in this, her special year, and knowing I'd be away for Beating the Retreat, and also I could no longer stand at the pavement side, I booked two seats for the Windsor Horse Show on the Saturday. Linda, the actress I got into "Bohème", came with me, she's wonderfully supportive. We were lucky with the travelling, and once into the show ground, discovered there were buggies to ferry you around. We were given front row seats. And yes, Her Majesty showed up, and we saw her well, if distantly, presenting some of the prizes. She was in a shocking pink coat and matching hat, and I have a bright pink dot on a photo to prove I saw her! But the best part was the buggy ride back to the gates to go home. The girl driver said, "I'm going to give you a treat, the front entrance is all clogged-up, so I'm going to take you through the backstage area". We saw all the stabling and accommodation (the British looked ramshackle). There were horses just being horses, and squaddies scrabbling out of fancy uniforms and downing pints. But best of all was the Omani encampment, they'd built a palace, all painted green and purple, complete with minarets. They were just going into the arena, 100 men and horses were lined up in the road. We passed them, and of course I waved and they all waved back. Linda said, "They thought you were the Queen, Pamela", (a likeness to Her Madge has been remarked on, but alas, never exploited) and we laughed all the way back to Paddington. It was a wonderful day.

Next came my holiday in the Greek island of Santorini. I'd arranged to go for a week as I so wanted to see the Minoan city they'd excavated from the mountains of ash that had preserved it. Viewing Akrotiri had been on my bucket list for years. I stayed the night before I left with Sue in Wimbledon, and she was going to look after my present cat, Perdy. She drove me down to Gatwick at 4 a.m. and came with me as far as she was allowed at the Airport.

I had a wonderful tour of the Minoan city. A lady professor showed me round, taking photos on my iPad as we went. It was weird, walking down this High Street between two storey houses (with loos on the second floor – how's that for civilisation?) knowing people had shopped and gossiped there four thousand years ago. It was hard not to believe it was all one vast film set; I stretched out a hand, just to feel the reality of the stone walls, and was quickly reprimanded. It was a wonderful and always to be remembered visit.

My holiday was somewhat marred, when, barefoot, I slipped on a few drops of water on the bathroom floor, cracking my back against the marble bath as I went down. I was quite alone on this holiday, and as I was in pain, I spent the next day lying on the bed. Unfortunately, the weather broke, so I filled the rest of my week with visits to the two splendid museums.

Although I had wheelchairs, the journey home jolted my back into spasm. The doctor didn't seem inclined to see me; and I spent another week lying on my own bed. (The TV was very entertaining; Murray was at Queens and the Queen was at Ascot). Eventually my back was x-rayed and the verdict was I hadn't done any real damage, (wrong!) but I'd just led a rather rough 85 years (right!).

Then my agent actually got me an audition. Usually people aren't prepared to pay the high price for the required Insurance at our age. Judi Dench – yes, unknown Binns – no. But this one was for a Granny at a big family party. All she had to do was fall forward into a large chocolate cake. The day before the audition I thought I'd better just practice bending forward from the waist. I did – and my back went off into spasm again and of course I couldn't go. So when my agent came up with another audition she was sceptical about my attending, especially as it entailed pretending to play the organ. But I insisted – I get so few chances nowadays. I didn't dare try out my mime, but worked out in my head exactly what I was going to do, and doped myself to the eyeballs with painkillers. After the audition I was so far gone I wandered about the West End for hours. When I got home I found I'd been pencilled in for the commercial. If I got it, I'd be flying to the Ukraine the following Monday.

After an excruciating wait I heard I'd got the part – The Music Mistress. The commercial was for T.K. Maxx, and was called "Ridiculous Possibilities". I was bidden to a Wardrobe call on the top floor of the T.K. Maxx in Denmark Street. I was given a warm welcome by their Wardrobe Mistress, Rachel Davis. I met the delightful Richard Adkins, he supervised everything. I tried on lots and lots of different get-ups, but what I would wear in the commercial was left undecided.

Richard Adkins made all the arrangements with my agent. He was at Heathrow, with a wheelchair, to meet me, very early in the morning on the day of our flight to Kiev. (They were making the commercial in the Ukraine as there was a great deal of complicated machinery, including the machinery which would make the organ rotate as I pretended to play. The technicians there were highly skilled and cheaper than those in the U.K.)

Once we arrived at Boryspil Airport, a taxi whisked me to the Grand Fairmont Hotel. It seemed as big as Versailles, I never even found the dining room. I wasn't given any time to unpack, another car took me to a rather grand dinner, which I really didn't want. I'd much enjoyed the food on the plane, now I gathered none of the production staff had eaten it. We all sat round a long table, shaded from the sun, and presided over by Mrs. Funk, the American head of T.K. Maxx. It was a very hot afternoon, I was interested that she was wearing a thick mustard wool polo-necked jumper under a bronzy-brown wool pinafore dress. Her legs were bare, she had flat Greek sandals with thonging right up to her knees.

As I wasn't eating much, I was sent away early. I was put in yet another car, I became a bit alarmed when no-one else got in with me. The driver didn't speak English. I had no idea where I was going. The car stopped in a kind of courtyard. Several people seemed to be expecting me – I was led up flights of stone steps and through several open-plan offices. At last a face I knew: Rachel Davis, the Wardrobe Mistress, was there to greet me. I was to try on all the costumes – brought from London, all over again. A couple of screens had been put up to make a rather inadequate changing area. I put my handbag under the one chair, there was nowhere else. As I hadn't had a chance to unpack, my tablet was still in it. Sometime during the evening my tablet was taken from the bag. A long time later, Richard Adkins very kindly reimbursed me.

All the different heads of T.K. Maxx, who'd been at the dinner, were now sitting in a half circle. I had to go out in each different costume and show it to them, together with a short piece of my 'pretending to play the organ' mime. The hours passed, and it grew very wearying. The man from Germany, who I'd sat next to at the dinner, and immediately liked, saw I was getting tired (I'd had breakfast at 4 a.m.) and called out, "You look beautiful, Pamela, whatever you're wearing". That was wonderfully cheering. At last it was decided my costume was to be grey trousers, a white roll-neck silk sweater, and a red cardie – as I was the Ring Mistress of this circus-style commercial.

But that wasn't the end of my exhausting day. A Ukrainian youth, one of my two chaperones, had to accompany me back to the hotel to thoroughly search my room to make sure the tablet had well and truly vanished. When, finally, I was alone, I found the bed was so high I couldn't climb into it. I had to make stepping stones with chairs culled from various parts of my suite before I could at last rest my weary head.

I'd been told to be in the hotel foyer by 9.00am the next morning. I met Sasha – a dear little Ukrainian drama student, who was my other chaperone. Apparently, I had the day off. It seemed Sarah Vignot, the girl who was coming from Paris to do wonderful tricks on her motorbike, while I pretended to accompany her to the strains of the Waltz from 'The Sleeping Beauty", had missed her connection in Vienna and wouldn't arrive for another twenty-four hours. I also learnt that Mrs. Funk was very kindly lending me her Rolls-Royce and her chauffeur for the day.

Sasha asked what I'd like to do? I'd caught sight of many golden domes among the trees sloping down to the river from the car that brought me from the airport. I asked to see all the thirteenth-century churches. So we had a wonderful morning going from one gold-encrusted interior to the next. For our afternoon's sightseeing, anxious to avoid all the heavy Russian Communist statuary, I chose to go to the Holy Caves of Lavra. These man-made caverns are where people came, through the centuries, to starve themselves nearly to the point of death to achieve a state of High Spirituality. It was rather gruesome crawling through the caverns past all the coffins holding the fully-clothed skeletons. It is considered such a Holy site that people still come over from Russia to pray, and kiss the coffins. Sasha said I'd been very brave as I despatched her to buy cans of Sprite to revive us.

The next day was the filming of the commercial. We were driven to the trailers parked at the edge of a vast car park. Men with guns patrolled the perimeters. The French girl, Sarah, had been there since dawn, taming and preparing her motorbike on which she would perform these wondrous tricks.

I was introduced to my tiny shiny pale blue organ. My first thought was 'no handles'. There was nothing to hold on to, just a built in seat with no back. The first time I tried it, whoever was controlling the rotating movement turned it up to full strength, and I was very nearly thrown right across the car park. It seemed it was double the speed I was supposed to go!

Sarah began to demonstrate her tricks – she stood on the saddle as she whizzed past me, her arms outstretched and hair flying. I gathered the bike didn't always do what she wanted, it was almost as temperamental as a horse. So the filming was a bit chancy, the crew had to nab their shots

291

when they could. Sarah was incredible the way she controlled the heavy bike, she was slim and slight, not at all brawny and butch, and pink and white like a dairymaid. I found I could pick up her thoughts quite easily, and we worked well together. My proudest moment came when the very grand cameraman – he wore a dapper Panama hat and a blazer and wouldn't speak to anyone in the car in the mornings, clapped his hands and said he had an announcement to make. His voice was like the late Brian Sewell's, and he said, "I want to tell everyone that Pamela's technique flows down my lens like liquid gold". There was some desultory clapping, and I thanked Heaven for my little bit of E.S.P. Everyone seemed very pleased with the filming. The commercial was a huge success, it was shown for four months and had the added accolade of being in cinemas, too.

In the morning Sasha came with me to Boryspil Airport. I was flying home alone as the production team were staying on to make another commercial (never heard of again). Sasha was very upset when she heard my plane, coming from London, was delayed by a few hours. She couldn't stay with me, but she got me a wheelchair, and we said a tearful 'goodbye'. I was wheeled away; once more not knowing where I was going. I was parked in what I took to be the Departure Lounge. There was plenty of free food, but I wasn't hungry. No-one spoke English – why should they? I was worried that I wouldn't understand the announcement when my plane did turn up. But all was well, and I was safely delivered to the BA Stewardesses.

CHAPTER TWENTY

My sex scene
didn't win a prize at Cannes,
but I was eighty-five

2016

Although the plane had been delayed, and I was a bit jet lagged, it was the best possible homecoming. There was a message from my agent saying there was a job waiting – three days filming the following week, if I wasn't too tired (!!! jobbing actresses are never too tired if there's work about). I read the script of "Elderflower" eagerly. The leads were to be played by Lou Sanders, she'd written it with Hannah George, and Tom Rosenthal, who'd very kindly recommended me for the part of Ivy. There were two other old lady rôles, to be taken by Sheila Reid, who I'd often seen on TV, and Ingrid Evans, who I knew slightly from Equity Branch Meetings.

It was a good story. These three old ladies take on a flower shop, which quickly starts to lose money. They discover that previously it had been a brothel. In order to avoid bankruptcy, they become amateur tarts. I was pleased to see that my character was the first to achieve a pick-up. Then there was a bedroom scene. Horrified, I read the words, "She straddles him". "Oh no, she doesn't", I thought. Furious that she'd agreed to this on my behalf, I was on the phone to my agent before a cat could swallow a sardine. Of course Jackie hadn't read the script, and professed herself 'horrified'. There was a lot of parlaying with lovely Gina Lyons, who ran Porcelain Films and was producing. Finally I graciously agreed to be shot cuddling up to the unlucky man, to be played by Marek Larwood.

It was a very low budget film, and many of the old ladies' scenes were filmed in a tiny 'Larkspur and Lavender' flower shop they'd found in Victoria Road, East London. It had an equally minute bathroom, where we all changed. I couldn't even reach to see the mirror. Sharing a car with Sheila going home one night, she asked, "Pamela, where were you made up the first day?" "In the street", I replied truthfully. Sheila nearly fell out of the car laughing. I had not been impressed by the professional make-up lady. I doubted she'd ever had to put a wig on before. (I was wearing my own). She didn't attempt to pin up my shoulder length hair, just dumped the wig on top, so I looked like a two-tiered cake. Between takes Sheila tried to loop some of the straying tendrils behind my ears, without much success. When Ben Mallaby, the director, wanted a queue of extras pretending to be lining up for our brothel, he stopped passers-by in the street and filmed them, all blithely unaware of what they were supposed to be queuing for. But the scene came out very convincingly.

I was led to the bedroom where *the* scene was to be shot. Ben had been thrilled that I possessed a rather gaudy kimono, bought many years ago from a cheap catalogue. The lovely comedy actor, Marek Larwood, was already lying on the double bed. The lights and the camera were in readiness. I turned to our wonderful director, "Ben", I said, "If I do IT, will it make the film funnier?" We knew Gina was intending to enter "Elderflower" for the Cannes Festival, and of course we were all rooting for its success.

Ben looked at me, and spoke seriously: "Pamela, if you do it, it will be hilarious". He added, "You can practice on me if you like –". That clinched it, Ben was young, slim and attractive, and I really enjoyed my rehearsal. Straddling the porky Marek was very different. The poor man had to physically support me in position while I kept whispering desperately how we'd hit Hollywood like a second Burton and Taylor. And then 'twas done, and done quickly. I'd achieved my first and only sex scene, and I was eighty five years old.

Lovely Gina wanted all her 'ladies' to have a car to their première, so I arrived in style, but was shattered to find a large paying audience at the basement venue. It costs £1,000 to enter a film for Cannes, and the tickets had been sold to fund this. I'd asked if my friend Sue could come, and when I arrived, she was already there, chatting to Gina as if they were old friends. I'd wanted someone there to hide behind if I got too embarrassed. But Ben had shot my scene so cleverly the audience were left rubbing their eyes and wondering if they'd really seen what they'd thought they saw. A lovely film with such lovely people. A thoroughly enjoyable experience.

My agent told me she'd got me a day's filming with Olly Murs. "Who's he?", I asked, in the same way I had to enquire about Ashton Kutcher on being told I was to be his Granny, the previous year.

I was informed a good half of the world was mad for Olly Murs, that he was the pop star of the moment and his records were selling in their millions. That satisfied my curiosity, and I couldn't wait to meet him. In the early morning of the day I was to film with Olly Murs, I was waiting for the call to tell me the car had arrived. Both the landline and the mobile remained sullenly silent. I thought I heard a tinkle that might have been the front doorbell. I headed off down the fifty stairs at half-tilt (I don't do full) and out into the darkness. The street was full of parked cars but otherwise deserted. Bereft of the landline, I was desperate. I invoked the help of the only passer-by – a little Chinese girl. I got her to phone my agent on her mobile. With iron in her voice, Jackie commanded me to return to my sofa. Eventually it was through the morning rush hour traffic that I was conveyed to the Wimbledon hangar where the filming was taking place.

I was a bit upset by all the no-car business, but the P.A. who greeted me was kindness itself.

She suggested I made my base on a large comfortable sofa in the vestibule, rather than climbing all the way up to the dressing rooms. My hair and make-up were checked, and also my get-up. (We'd all been told to wear black and white). From far off I could hear Olly's recorded voice. The video we were all there to film with him was "Years and Years". Once or twice I peeped through the double doors into the studio, but I could only see a lot of people standing around. The nice P.A. gave me a ticket for lunch. Towards one o'clock people began to drift from the studio to a door on my left. That must be the way to the canteen. The studio doors were flung open and Olly and his entourage emerged. The leaders swept past me, but Olly stopped. He must have seen a very old actress with her stick propped beside her. He proffered his hand. "I'm Olly", he said in a matter-of-fact way. I took his hand and said, "Pamela". A broad smile lit up his round boyish face. He repeated my name, pronouncing every syllable carefully – "Pam-eel-la", before being hurried away by his aides. I noticed he was wearing very ordinary jeans and a white T. Eventually I located the restaurant, and loaded a very good meal onto my tray. The large room was light and airy, and there were posies of flowers on all the tables. I positioned myself where I could see Mr. Murs, I so wanted to get a photo of him. When I decided it was time to return to my sofa, I made for the lift. And there was Olly, smiling and again repeating my name. Seizing my moment, I asked for a photo, to which the Pop Idol readily agreed, putting his arm round my waist. I handed my little camera – it was the kind you have to wind on after every shot, to some girl, and she went click! click! click! so alas all the shots were melded together and I never got my Olly photo. But he escorted me, arm-in-arm, from the lift, and saw me comfortably installed back on my sofa.

I was placed nowhere near the star throughout the filming. We – there was a large range of age and ethnicity among the actors, were shot in various lines and various positions about the set. And every so often Olly would shoot up his hand and wave and carol out my name, much to my embarrassment and curious stares from everyone else. There was one shot where all the actors had to walk past the camera in a long straight line. Since the valgus I was left with after the cramp attacks makes my walking rather odd, I was barred from this scene. For once I became very aware of my disability. All the time Olly's recorded song was belting out, and we watched him beautifully mime love scenes with a young actress. During breaks he turned cartwheels with the kids, who all adored him.

They even gave us supper. I was enjoying mine, from a tray, in a corner when Olly came to record a spoken message to go with the video. He kept fluffing, but that didn't bother him. The sound recordist asked for yet another take. Olly complied, flashing me an impish grin, and saying "this one's for Pamela"... He certainly made my day, with his impeccable manners and clear enjoyment of life. Who would begrudge the sale of millions of records to such an endearing young man who'd made the day for one very old actress?

My agent, Jackie, had an email from the Casting Director for Helen O'Hanlon, saying Helen had seen my photos and was considering me for a small part in her next film "Mirette on the High Wire". Would I, they wondered, consider attending a general audition?

With some trepidation, I said I'd go. It sounded as if they'd all be wearing jeans, and we'd be expected to lie on the floor. I don't do either, and I had to hire a car to get to the pub venue as it didn't seem to be near any discernible bus routes. (It wasn't). They sent me a copy of the script beforehand, it was adapted from the American children's book by Emily Arnold McCully.

The audition wasn't as bad as I expected. There were about forty people there, and we all sang and danced for over an hour. There were tables and chairs, laid out like a café, and copies of the song from the film, printed in a very large font, stuck to the tables, so there was no excuse for not knowing the words. I danced the whole time, not being much of a singist. I noticed an actor who seemed rather out of things. I joined up with him, and he twirled me round and we did a lot of eighteenth-century bowing and curtseying. Two days later I heard I'd been given a part: I was to be one of two Old Show Girls. The other was to be played by Jacqui Chan. Only one other actor, as well as me, got into the film from that audition.

The fittings were at the National Theatre

Costume Hire Store, near The Oval. Another actress, Katie Carr, very kindly drove me there. I tried to help her find an agent. I suggested she contacted John Colclough. When I was recovering from the Covent Garden accident, my then agent, Simon Cutting, sadly told me he was leaving the business. At the time I was wondering if I would ever work again; this news seemed the very last straw. But when I was better and thinking of getting another agent, someone at Spotlight suggested I contacted John Colclough and he sent me to see the splendid Jackie Williamson. I've been with her ever since.

I'd imagined for the film I'd look like a Degas on a bad day, in an over-long rather grubby tutu. Instead I got a ravishingly flattering eau-de-nil evening dress, with fluttering swansdown round the neckline and the sleeves. The period was 1912. I hadn't had such a gorgeous cozzie for years. We were all variety performers living in a Paris boarding house. This was kept by Miriam Margolyes and her grand-daughter, Mirette of the title, delightfully played by Dixie Egerickx. Despite the nose-picking and the farting, I was glad we had Miriam on board, apart from being a wonderful actress, she led the company very ably and got us all going. The same could not be said of Tom Conti, apart from giving a beautiful performance as the Theatrical Agent, he rather withdrew into the shadows. I learnt later he was having trouble selling his house at the time.

We had one day's rehearsal in some old building down in the City. After arriving, I paused before entering the ancient high-beamed room. What I saw could have been taking place any time in the last four hundred years: someone was playing the piano while someone else sang. In a corner a jester was juggling. A ventriloquist was unpacking his doll, and a young girl was practising handstands. Truly, "the players had come".

The main part of the filming was done in a pub, the George Tavern on the Commercial Road. It was built in 1600. In a large room on the top floor, the plaster had been stripped back to reveal beams and there was a huge Tudor fireplace. It made a perfect setting for the parlour of the boarding house. For this film a special new form of colour photography was being used. Before each "take" the set was flooded with dry-ice fumes, it was like acting in a fog. I saw some of the rushes and the results were magical: the colours of the so-carefully-selected costumes came up like jewels. At the time we were shooting these scenes, Dixie was learning to wire walk. She had her own wire, about two foot off the ground, to practise on in her garden at home. She proudly told me she could manage nine steps without falling off. She was such a determined little actress I had no doubts that she'd be able to do the full length of the wire when these scenes were shot in France the following Spring. The fascinating Jean-Marie Desmond, who was playing Bellini, the Houdini character, came over for one day. He told me he'd been going to the gym in Paris three times a week. Proudly he showed me a video on his phone; not only could he walk the entire length of the wire, but he was confident enough to crouch right down. I was much looking forward to seeing these scenes which would close the film.

Meanwhile, I was having to cope with four flights of Tudor stairs, and the long train of my dress. I insisted on going down to the bar in the basement for lunch. I looked up at the carved oak pillars, standing as they had done for four hundred years. I realised Shakespeare could have leant against them, he'd surely have popped in for an ale after his performances. Such a wonderful production with such lovely people. It was a perfect ending to my magical year, bringing the past right up to the present. Christmas was coming, and I was walking AND working.

37003801R00170

Printed in Poland
by Amazon Fulfillment
Poland Sp. z o.o., Wrocław